Made | Simple™
ITALIAN

pil

Publications International, Ltd.

Made Simple is a trademark of Publications International, Ltd.

Pictured on the front cover: Vegetable Penne Italiano *(page 100)*.

Pictured on the back cover *(clockwise from top):* Beans and Greens Crostini *(page 28)*, Braised Short Ribs in Red Wine *(page 118)* and Tiramisu *(page 173)*.

ISBN: 978-1-64030-864-0

Manufactured in China.

8 7 6 5 4 3 2 1

Microwave Cooking: Microwave ovens vary in wattage. Use the cooking times as guidelines and check for doneness before adding more time.

WARNING: Food preparation, baking and cooking involve inherent dangers: misuse of electric products, sharp electric tools, boiling water, hot stoves, allergic reactions, foodborne illnesses and the like, pose numerous potential risks. Publications International, Ltd. (PIL) assumes no responsibility or liability for any damages you may experience as a result of following recipes, instructions, tips or advice in this publication.

While we hope this publication helps you find new ways to eat delicious foods, you may not always achieve the results desired due to variations in ingredients, cooking temperatures, typos, errors, omissions or individual cooking abilities.

Let's get social!
 @Publications_International
@PublicationsInternational
www.pilcookbooks.com

TABLE OF CONTENTS

APPETIZERS

NO-FUSS CAPONATA

makes about 5¼ cups

1 medium eggplant (about 1 pound), peeled and cut into ½-inch pieces

1 can (about 14 ounces) diced Italian plum tomatoes

1 onion, chopped

1 red bell pepper, cut into ½-inch pieces

½ cup mild salsa

¼ cup olive oil

2 tablespoons capers, drained

2 tablespoons balsamic vinegar

3 cloves garlic, minced

1 teaspoon dried oregano

½ teaspoon salt

⅓ cup packed fresh basil, cut into thin strips

Toasted bread slices (optional)

SLOW COOKER DIRECTIONS

1. Combine eggplant, tomatoes, onion, bell pepper, salsa, oil, capers, vinegar, garlic, oregano and salt in slow cooker; mix well.

2. Cover; cook on LOW 7 to 8 hours. Stir in basil. Serve at room temperature on bread slices, if desired.

MARINATED ANTIPASTO

makes about 5 cups

¼ cup extra virgin olive oil

2 tablespoons balsamic vinegar

1 clove garlic, minced

½ teaspoon salt

¼ teaspoon black pepper

1 pint (2 cups) cherry or grape tomatoes

1 can (about 14 ounces) quartered artichoke hearts, drained

8 ounces small balls or cubes fresh mozzarella cheese

1 cup drained pitted kalamata olives

¼ cup sliced fresh basil leaves

Lettuce leaves

1. Whisk oil, vinegar, garlic, salt and pepper in medium bowl. Add tomatoes, artichokes, mozzarella, olives and basil; toss to coat. Let stand at room temperature 30 minutes.

2. Line platter with lettuce. Arrange antipasto over lettuce; serve at room temperature.

SERVING SUGGESTION: Serve antipasto with toothpicks as an appetizer or spoon over Bibb lettuce leaves on individual plates for a first-course salad.

CAPRESE PIZZA

makes 6 servings

1 **loaf (16 ounces) frozen pizza or bread dough, thawed**

1 **container (12 ounces) bruschetta sauce**

1 **container (8 ounces) pearl-size fresh mozzarella cheese (perlini), drained***

*If pearl-size mozzarella is not available, use one (8-ounce) ball of fresh mozzarella and chop into ¼-inch pieces.

1. Preheat oven to 400°F. Spray baking sheet with nonstick cooking spray.

2. Roll out dough into 15×10-inch rectangle on lightly floured surface. Transfer to prepared baking sheet. Cover loosely with plastic wrap; let rest 10 minutes. Meanwhile, place bruschetta sauce in colander; let drain 10 minutes.

3. Prick surface of dough several times with fork. Bake 10 minutes. Spread drained bruschetta sauce over crust; top with cheese. Bake 10 minutes or until cheese is melted and crust is golden brown. Serve warm.

NOTE: Bruschetta sauce is a mixture of diced fresh tomatoes, garlic, basil and olive oil. It is typically found in the refrigerated section of the supermarket with other prepared dips such as hummus.

TUSCAN WHITE BEAN CROSTINI

makes 18 crostini

2 cans (about 15 ounces each) cannellini or Great Northern beans, rinsed and drained

½ large red bell pepper, finely chopped *or* ⅓ cup finely chopped roasted red bell pepper

⅓ cup finely chopped onion

⅓ cup red wine vinegar

3 tablespoons chopped fresh parsley

1 tablespoon extra virgin olive oil

2 cloves garlic, minced

½ teaspoon dried oregano

¼ teaspoon black pepper

18 slices French bread, about ¼ inch thick

1. Combine beans, bell pepper and onion in large bowl; mix well.

2. Whisk vinegar, parsley, oil, garlic, oregano and black pepper in small bowl until blended. Pour over bean mixture; toss to coat. Cover and refrigerate 2 hours or overnight.

3. Preheat broiler. Arrange bread slices in single layer on ungreased baking sheet or broiler pan. Broil 6 to 8 inches from heat 30 to 45 seconds or until lightly toasted. Cool completely.

4. Top each toasted bread slice with scant 3 tablespoons bean mixture.

MOZZARELLA AND PROSCIUTTO BITES

makes 16 to 20 pieces

16 to 20 small bamboo skewers or toothpicks

8 ounces fresh mozzarella

¼ cup chopped fresh basil

½ teaspoon black pepper

6 to 8 thin slices prosciutto

1. Soak skewers in water 20 minutes to prevent burning. Cut cheese into 1- to 1½-inch chunks.* Place on paper towel-lined plate; sprinkle with basil and pepper, turning to coat all sides.

2. Cut prosciutto slices crosswise into thirds. Tightly wrap one slice prosciutto around each piece of mozzarella, covering completely. Insert skewer into each piece. Freeze skewers 15 minutes to firm.

3. Preheat broiler. Line broiler pan or baking sheet with foil. Place skewers on prepared pan; broil about 3 minutes or until prosciutto begins to crisp, turning once. Serve immediately.

You can substitute one 8-ounce container of small fresh mozzarella balls (ciliengini) for the larger piece of mozzarella. One 8-ounce container contains 24 balls.

RED PEPPER ANTIPASTO

makes 6 to 8 servings

1 tablespoon olive oil

3 red bell peppers, cut into 2×¼-inch strips

2 cloves garlic, minced

2 tablespoons red wine vinegar

¼ teaspoon salt

Black pepper

1. Heat oil in large skillet over medium-high heat. Add bell peppers; cook and stir 8 to 9 minutes or until edges of peppers begin to brown. Reduce heat to medium. Add garlic; cook and stir 1 minute.

2. Stir in vinegar, salt and black pepper; cook 2 minutes or until liquid has evaporated. Serve warm or at room temperature.

RED PEPPER CROSTINI: Brush thin slices of French bread with olive oil. Place on baking sheet; bake in preheated 350°F oven 10 minutes or until golden brown. Top with spoonfuls of Red Pepper Antipasto.

BALSAMIC ONION AND PROSCIUTTO PIZZETTES

makes 16 pizzettes

1 package (16 ounces) refrigerated pizza dough*

2 tablespoons extra virgin olive oil, divided

1 large *or* 2 small red onions, cut in half and thinly sliced

¼ teaspoon salt

1½ tablespoons balsamic vinegar

⅛ teaspoon black pepper

⅔ cup grated Parmesan cheese

4 ounces fresh mozzarella, cut into small pieces

1 package (about 3 ounces) thinly sliced prosciutto, cut or torn into small pieces

Frozen pizza dough can also be used. Thaw according to package directions.

1. Remove dough from refrigerator; let rest at room temperature while preparing onions. Heat 1 tablespoon oil in large skillet over medium-high heat. Add onion and salt; cook about 20 minutes or until tender and golden brown, stirring occasionally. Add vinegar and pepper; cook and stir 2 minutes. Set aside to cool.

2. Preheat oven to 450°F. Line two baking sheets with parchment paper.

3. Divide dough into 16 balls; press into 3-inch rounds (about ⅜ inch thick) on prepared baking sheets. Brush rounds with remaining 1 tablespoon oil; sprinkle each round with about 1 teaspoon Parmesan. Top with cooked onion, mozzarella, prosciutto and remaining Parmesan.

4. Bake about 13 minutes or until crusts are golden brown.

BRUSCHETTA

makes 8 servings

4 plum tomatoes, seeded and diced

½ cup packed fresh basil leaves, finely chopped

5 tablespoons extra virgin olive oil, divided

2 cloves garlic, minced

¼ teaspoon salt

⅛ teaspoon black pepper

16 slices Italian bread

2 tablespoons grated Parmesan cheese

1. Combine fresh tomatoes, basil, 3 tablespoons oil, garlic, salt and pepper in large bowl; mix well. Let stand at room temperature 1 hour.

2. Preheat oven to 375°F. Place bread on baking sheet. Brush remaining 2 tablespoons oil over one side of bread slices; sprinkle with cheese. Bake 6 to 8 minutes or until toasted.

3. Top each bread slice with 1 tablespoon tomato mixture.

GOAT CHEESE-STUFFED FIGS >

makes 7 servings

7 fresh firm ripe figs

7 slices prosciutto

1 package (4 ounces) goat cheese
   Ground black pepper

1. Preheat broiler. Line baking sheet with foil. Cut figs in half vertically. Cut prosciutto slices in half lengthwise to create 14 pieces (about 4 inches long and 1 inch wide).

2. Spread 1 teaspoon goat cheese onto cut side of each fig half. Wrap prosciutto slice around fig and goat cheese; sprinkle with pepper.

3. Broil about 4 minutes or until cheese softens and figs are heated through.

OYSTERS ROMANO

makes 12 oysters

12 oysters, shucked and on the half
    shell

2 slices bacon, each cut into 6 pieces

½ cup Italian seasoned dry bread
    crumbs

2 tablespoons butter, melted

½ teaspoon garlic salt

6 tablespoons grated Romano
    or Parmesan cheese
   Fresh chives (optional)

1. Preheat oven to 375°F. Place shells with oysters on baking sheet. Top each oyster with one bacon piece. Bake 10 minutes or until bacon is crisp.

2. Combine bread crumbs, butter and garlic salt in small bowl; mix well. Spoon mixture over oysters; sprinkle with cheese. Bake 5 minutes or until cheese is melted. Garnish with chives.

MOZZARELLA IN CARROZZA

makes about 8 servings

2 eggs

⅓ cup milk

¼ teaspoon salt

⅛ teaspoon black pepper

8 slices country Italian bread

6 ounces fresh mozzarella, cut into ¼-inch slices

8 oil-packed sun-dried tomatoes, drained and cut into strips

8 to 12 fresh basil leaves, torn

1½ tablespoons olive oil

1. Whisk eggs, milk, salt and pepper in shallow bowl or baking dish until well blended.

2. Place four bread slices on work surface. Top with cheese, sun-dried tomatoes, basil and remaining bread slices.

3. Heat oil in large skillet over medium heat. Dip sandwiches in egg mixture, turning and pressing to coat completely. Add sandwiches to skillet; cook 5 minutes per side or until golden brown. Cut into strips or squares.

TIP: To serve these sandwiches as a snack or lunch instead of an appetizer, cut them into halves instead of strips.

PEPPERONATA

makes 4 servings

1 tablespoon extra virgin olive oil

4 large red, yellow and/or orange
   bell peppers, cut into thin strips

2 cloves garlic, coarsely chopped

12 pimiento-stuffed green olives or
   pitted black olives, cut into halves

2 to 3 tablespoons white or red
   wine vinegar

¼ teaspoon salt

¼ teaspoon black pepper

1. Heat oil in large skillet over medium-high heat. Add bell peppers; cook 8 to 9 minutes or until edges begin to brown, stirring frequently.

2. Reduce heat to medium. Add garlic; cook and stir 1 to 2 minutes. (Do not allow garlic to brown.) Add olives, vinegar, salt and black pepper; cook 1 to 2 minutes or until all liquid has evaporated.

NOTE: Pepperonata is a very versatile dish. It can be chilled and served as part of an antipasti selection. It can also be served warm as a condiment or as a side with meat dishes.

ASPARAGUS AND PROSCIUTTO ANTIPASTO

makes 12 appetizers

12 asparagus spears (about 8 ounces)

2 ounces cream cheese, softened

¼ cup crumbled blue cheese or goat cheese

¼ teaspoon black pepper

1 package (3 to 4 ounces) thinly sliced prosciutto

1. Trim and discard tough ends of asparagus spears. Simmer asparagus in salted water in large skillet 4 to 5 minutes or until crisp-tender. Drain and rinse under cold water until cool. Pat dry with paper towels.

2. Combine cream cheese, blue cheese and pepper in small bowl; mix well. Cut prosciutto slices in half crosswise to make 12 pieces. Spread cream cheese mixture evenly over one side of each prosciutto slice.

3. Wrap each asparagus spear with prosciutto slice. Serve at room temperature or slightly chilled.

BEANS AND GREENS CROSTINI

makes about 24 crostini

4 tablespoons olive oil, divided

1 small onion, thinly sliced

4 cups thinly sliced Italian black kale or other dinosaur kale variety

2 tablespoons minced garlic, divided

1 tablespoon balsamic vinegar

2 teaspoons salt, divided

¼ teaspoon red pepper flakes

1 can (about 15 ounces) cannellini beans, rinsed and drained

1 tablespoon chopped fresh rosemary

Toasted baguette slices

1. Heat 1 tablespoon oil in large skillet over medium heat. Add onion; cook and stir 3 minutes or until softened. Add kale and 1 tablespoon garlic; cook 15 minutes or until kale is softened and most liquid has evaporated, stirring occasionally. Stir in vinegar, 1 teaspoon salt and red pepper flakes.

2. Meanwhile, combine beans, remaining 3 tablespoons oil, 1 tablespoon garlic, 1 teaspoon salt and rosemary in food processor or blender; process until smooth.

3. Spread baguette slices with bean mixture; top with kale.

SOUPS

ITALIAN FISH SOUP

makes 2 servings

1 cup meatless pasta sauce

¾ cup water

¾ cup chicken broth

1 teaspoon Italian seasoning

¾ cup uncooked small pasta shells

4 ounces fresh halibut or haddock steak, 1 inch thick, skinned and cut into 1-inch pieces

1½ cups frozen vegetable blend, such as broccoli, carrots and cauliflower

1. Combine pasta sauce, water, broth and Italian seasoning in medium saucepan; bring to a boil over high heat. Stir in pasta; return to a boil. Reduce heat to medium-low; cover and simmer 5 minutes.

2. Stir in fish and frozen vegetables; return to a boil. Reduce heat to medium-low; cover and simmer 4 to 5 minutes or until pasta is tender and fish begins to flake when tested with fork.

HEARTY WHITE BEAN MINESTRONE

makes 6 to 8 servings

2 medium russet potatoes (about 6 ounces each), peeled and cut into ½-inch pieces

3 medium carrots, chopped

3 medium stalks celery, chopped

1 medium onion, chopped

2 cloves garlic, minced

5 cups vegetable broth

2 cans (about 15 ounces each) cannellini beans, rinsed and drained

1 can (about 14 ounces) diced tomatoes

6 cups chopped fresh kale

⅓ cup shredded Parmesan cheese (optional)

SLOW COOKER DIRECTIONS

1. Combine potatoes, carrots, celery, onion and garlic in slow cooker. Stir in broth, beans and tomatoes; mix well.

2. Cover; cook on LOW 7 hours. Stir in kale. *Turn slow cooker to HIGH.* Cover; cook on HIGH 1 to 2 hours or until vegetables are tender.

3. Top with cheese, if desired.

PASTA E FAGIOLI

makes 8 servings

2 tablespoons olive oil

1 cup chopped onion

3 cloves garlic, minced

2 cans (about 14 ounces each) Italian-style stewed tomatoes, undrained

3 cups reduced-sodium chicken broth

1 can (about 15 ounces) cannellini beans,* undrained

¼ cup chopped fresh Italian parsley

1 teaspoon dried basil

¼ teaspoon black pepper

4 ounces uncooked small shell pasta

If cannellini beans are unavailable, substitute Great Northern beans.

1. Heat oil in large saucepan over medium heat. Add onion and garlic; cook and stir 5 minutes or until onion is tender.

2. Add tomatoes, broth, beans with liquid, parsley, basil and pepper to saucepan; bring to a boil over high heat, stirring occasionally. Reduce heat to low; cover and simmer 10 minutes.

3. Stir in pasta; cover and simmer 10 minutes or just until pasta is tender. Serve immediately.

HEARTY TUSCAN SOUP

makes 6 to 8 servings

1 teaspoon olive oil

1 pound bulk mild or hot Italian sausage*

1 medium onion, chopped

3 cloves garlic, minced

¼ cup all-purpose flour

5 cups chicken broth

1 teaspoon salt

½ teaspoon Italian seasoning

3 medium unpeeled russet potatoes (about 1 pound), halved lengthwise and thinly sliced

2 cups packed torn stemmed kale leaves

1 cup half-and-half or whipping cream

Or use sausage links and remove from casings.

1. Heat oil in large saucepan or Dutch oven over medium-high heat. Add sausage; cook until sausage begins to brown, stirring to break up meat. Add onion and garlic; cook about 5 minutes or until onion is softened and sausage is browned, stirring occasionally.

2. Stir in flour until blended. Add broth, salt and Italian seasoning; bring to a boil. Stir in potatoes and kale. Reduce heat to medium-low; simmer 15 to 20 minutes or until potatoes are fork-tender.

3. Stir in half-and-half; reduce heat to low. Simmer about 5 minutes or until heated through.

SIMPLE RAVIOLI SOUP

makes 8 servings

8 ounces mild Italian sausage, casings removed

½ cup chopped onion

1 clove garlic, crushed

2 cans (about 14 ounces each) chicken broth

2 cups water

1 package (9 ounces) frozen mini cheese-filled ravioli

1 can (about 15 ounces) chickpeas, rinsed and drained

1 can (about 14 ounces) diced tomatoes

¾ teaspoon dried oregano

½ teaspoon black pepper

1 cup fresh baby spinach

Grated Parmesan cheese

1. Cook sausage, onion and garlic in large saucepan or Dutch oven over medium heat 5 minutes or until sausage is no longer pink, stirring to break up meat. Drain fat. Transfer to large bowl.

2. Add broth and water to saucepan; bring to a boil over medium-high heat. Add ravioli; cook 4 to 5 minutes or until tender. Stir in sausage mixture, chickpeas, tomatoes, oregano and pepper; cook until heated through. Stir in spinach; cook 1 minute or until wilted. Sprinkle with cheese.

ROMAN SPINACH SOUP

makes 8 servings

6 cups chicken broth

4 eggs, beaten

¼ cup grated Parmesan cheese

¼ cup minced fresh basil

2 tablespoons fresh lemon juice

1 tablespoon minced fresh parsley

¼ teaspoon white pepper

⅛ teaspoon ground nutmeg

8 cups packed fresh spinach, chopped

1. Heat broth to a boil in large saucepan over medium heat.

2. Beat eggs, cheese, basil, lemon juice, parsley, white pepper and nutmeg in small bowl until well blended.

3. Stir spinach into broth; cook 1 minute. Slowly pour egg mixture into broth mixture, whisking constantly so egg threads form. Cook 2 to 3 minutes or until egg is cooked. Serve immediately.

NOTE: Soup may look curdled.

PASTA SOUP WITH FENNEL

makes 6 servings

1 tablespoon olive oil

1 small fennel bulb, trimmed and chopped into ¼-inch pieces (about 1½ cups)

4 cloves garlic, minced

3 cups vegetable broth

1 cup uncooked small shell pasta

1 medium zucchini or yellow summer squash, cut into ½-inch chunks

1 can (about 14 ounces) Italian-seasoned diced tomatoes

¼ cup grated Romano or Parmesan cheese

¼ cup chopped fresh basil

Dash black pepper (optional)

1. Heat oil in large saucepan over medium heat. Add fennel; cook and stir 5 minutes. Add garlic; cook and stir 30 seconds. Add broth and pasta; bring to a boil over high heat. Reduce heat to low; simmer 5 minutes.

2. Stir in zucchini; simmer 5 to 7 minutes or until pasta and vegetables are tender.

3. Stir in tomatoes; cook until heated through. Top with cheese, basil and pepper, if desired.

PESTO TORTELLINI SOUP

makes 6 servings

1 package (9 ounces) refrigerated cheese tortellini

3 cans (about 14 ounces each) chicken or vegetable broth

1 jar (7 ounces) roasted red peppers, drained and thinly sliced

¾ cup frozen green peas

3 to 4 cups packed stemmed fresh spinach

1 to 2 tablespoons prepared pesto

Grated Parmesan cheese (optional)

1. Cook tortellini according to package directions; drain.

2. Meanwhile, heat broth to a boil in large saucepan over high heat. Add cooked tortellini, roasted peppers and peas; return to a boil. Reduce heat to medium; simmer 1 minute.

3. Remove from heat; stir in spinach and pesto. Garnish with cheese.

QUICK TUSCAN BEAN, TOMATO AND SPINACH SOUP

makes 4 servings

2 cans (about 14 ounces each) diced tomatoes with onions

1 can (about 14 ounces) chicken broth

2 teaspoons sugar

2 teaspoons dried basil

¾ teaspoon Worcestershire sauce

1 can (about 15 ounces) small white beans, rinsed and drained

3 ounces baby spinach or chopped stemmed fresh spinach

1 tablespoon extra virgin olive oil

1. Combine tomatoes, broth, sugar, basil and Worcestershire sauce in large saucepan or Dutch oven; bring to a boil over high heat. Reduce heat to low; simmer 10 minutes.

2. Stir in beans and spinach; cook 5 minutes or until spinach is tender.

3. Remove from heat; stir in oil just before serving.

PEPPERY SICILIAN CHICKEN SOUP

makes 8 to 10 servings

2 tablespoons olive oil

1 onion, chopped

1 green bell pepper, chopped

3 stalks celery, chopped

3 carrots, chopped

3 cloves garlic, minced

1 tablespoon salt

3 containers (32 ounces each) chicken broth

2 pounds boneless skinless chicken breasts

1 can (28 ounces) diced tomatoes

2 baking potatoes, peeled and cut into ¼-inch pieces

1 tablespoon ground black pepper

½ cup chopped fresh parsley

8 ounces uncooked ditalini pasta

1. Heat oil in large saucepan or Dutch oven over medium heat. Stir in onion, bell pepper, celery and carrots. Reduce heat to medium-low; cover and cook 10 to 15 minutes or until vegetables are tender but not browned, stirring occasionally. Stir in garlic and 1 tablespoon salt; cover and cook 5 minutes.

2. Stir in broth, chicken, tomatoes, potatoes and black pepper; bring to a boil. Reduce heat to low; cover and cook 1 hour.

3. Remove chicken to plate; set aside until cool enough to handle. Shred chicken and return to saucepan with parsley.

4. Meanwhile, cook pasta in large saucepan of boiling salted water 7 minutes (or 1 minute less than package directs for al dente). Drain pasta and add to soup. Taste and add additional salt, if desired.

ITALIAN WEDDING SOUP

makes 8 servings

MEATBALLS

- 2 **eggs**
- 6 **cloves garlic, minced, divided**
- 2 **teaspoons salt, divided**
- ⅛ **teaspoon black pepper**
- 1½ **pounds meat loaf mix (ground beef and pork)**
- ¾ **cup plain dry bread crumbs**
- ½ **cup grated Parmesan cheese**

SOUP

- 2 **tablespoons olive oil**
- 1 **onion, chopped**
- 2 **carrots, chopped**
- 2 **heads escarole or curly endive, coarsely chopped**
- 8 **cups chicken broth**
- 1 **can (about 14 ounces) Italian plum tomatoes, undrained, coarsely chopped**
- 3 **sprigs fresh thyme**
- ½ **teaspoon red pepper flakes**
- 1 **cup uncooked acini di pepe pasta**

1. For meatballs, beat eggs, 2 cloves garlic, 1 teaspoon salt and black pepper in large bowl until blended. Stir in meat loaf mix, bread crumbs and cheese; mix gently until well blended. Shape tablespoonfuls of meat mixture into 1-inch balls.

2. For soup, heat oil in large saucepan or Dutch oven over medium heat. Cook meatballs in batches 5 minutes or until browned. Remove to plate; set aside.

3. Add onion, carrots and remaining 4 cloves garlic to same saucepan; cook and stir 5 minutes or until onion is lightly browned. Add escarole; cook 2 minutes or until wilted. Stir in broth, tomatoes with liquid, thyme, remaining 1 teaspoon salt and red pepper flakes; bring to a boil over high heat. Reduce heat to medium-low; simmer 15 minutes.

4. Add meatballs and pasta to soup; return to a boil over high heat. Reduce heat to medium; cook 10 minutes or until pasta is tender. Remove and discard thyme sprigs before serving.

LENTIL SOUP

makes 6 to 8 servings

2 tablespoons olive oil, divided

2 medium onions, chopped

1½ teaspoons salt

4 cloves garlic, minced

¼ cup tomato paste

1 teaspoon dried oregano

½ teaspoon dried basil

¼ teaspoon dried thyme

¼ teaspoon black pepper

½ cup dry sherry or white wine

8 cups vegetable broth

2 cups water

3 carrots, cut into ½-inch pieces

2 cups dried lentils, rinsed and sorted

1 cup chopped fresh parsley

1 tablespoon balsamic vinegar

1. Heat 1 tablespoon oil in large saucepan or Dutch oven over medium heat. Add onions; cook 10 minutes, stirring occasionally. Add remaining 1 tablespoon oil and salt; cook 10 minutes or until onions are golden brown, stirring frequently.

2. Add garlic; cook and stir 1 minute. Add tomato paste, oregano, basil, thyme and pepper; cook and stir 1 minute. Stir in sherry; cook 30 seconds, scraping up browned bits from bottom of saucepan.

3. Stir in broth, water, carrots and lentils; cover and bring to a boil over high heat. Reduce heat to medium-low; simmer, partially covered, 30 minutes or until lentils are tender.

4. Remove from heat; stir in parsley and vinegar.

PASTA E CECI

makes 4 servings

4 tablespoons olive oil, divided

1 onion, chopped

1 carrot, chopped

1 clove garlic, minced

1 sprig fresh rosemary

1 teaspoon salt

1 can (28 ounces) whole tomatoes, drained and crushed (see Tip)

2 cups vegetable broth or water

1 can (about 15 ounces) chickpeas, undrained

1 bay leaf

⅛ teaspoon red pepper flakes

1 cup uncooked orecchiette pasta

Black pepper

Chopped fresh parsley or basil (optional)

1. Heat 3 tablespoons oil in large saucepan over medium-high heat. Add onion and carrot; cook 10 minutes or until vegetables are softened, stirring occasionally.

2. Add garlic, rosemary and 1 teaspoon salt; cook and stir 1 minute. Stir in tomatoes, broth, chickpeas with liquid, bay leaf and red pepper flakes. Transfer 1 cup mixture to food processor or blender; process until smooth. Return blended mixture to saucepan; bring to a boil.

3. Stir in pasta. Reduce heat to medium; cook 12 to 15 minutes or until pasta is tender. Remove and discard rosemary sprig and bay leaf. Taste and season with additional salt and pepper, if desired. Garnish with parsley; drizzle with remaining 1 tablespoon oil.

TIP: To crush the tomatoes, take them out of the can one at a time and crush them between your fingers over the pot. Or coarsely chop them with with a knife.

SALADS & SANDWICHES

ASPARAGUS AND ARUGULA SALAD

makes 4 to 6 servings

½ cup sun-dried tomatoes (not packed in oil)

1 cup boiling water

1 cup sliced asparagus (1-inch pieces)

1 package (5 ounces) baby arugula (4 cups)

½ cup shaved Parmesan cheese

¼ cup extra virgin olive oil

2 tablespoons lemon juice

1 tablespoon orange juice

1 clove garlic, minced

½ teaspoon salt

½ teaspoon grated lemon peel

⅛ teaspoon black pepper

1. Place sun-dried tomatoes in small bowl; cover with boiling water. Let stand 5 minutes; drain well.

2. Bring medium saucepan of salted water to a boil. Add asparagus; cook 1 minute or until crisp-tender. Rinse under cold running water to stop cooking.

3. Combine arugula, asparagus, sun-dried tomatoes and cheese in large bowl. Whisk oil, lemon juice, orange juice, garlic, salt, lemon peel and pepper in small bowl until well blended. Pour dressing over salad; toss gently to coat.

SPINACH AND ROASTED PEPPER PANINI >

makes 4 servings

1 loaf (12 ounces) focaccia

1½ cups fresh spinach leaves

1 jar (about 7 ounces) roasted red peppers, drained

4 ounces fontina cheese, thinly sliced

¾ cup thinly sliced red onion

Olive oil

1. Cut focaccia in half horizontally. Layer bottom half with spinach, roasted peppers, cheese and onion. Cover with top half of focaccia. Brush outsides of sandwich lightly with oil. Cut sandwich into four pieces.

2. Heat large nonstick skillet over medium heat. Add sandwiches; press down lightly with spatula or weigh down with plate. Cook sandwiches 4 to 5 minutes per side or until cheese melts and bread is golden brown.

CHOPPED ITALIAN SALAD

makes 4 to 6 servings

10 cups chopped romaine lettuce

1 can (about 15 ounces) chickpeas, rinsed and drained

20 slices pepperoni, quartered

½ cup sliced or chopped black olives

⅓ cup chopped red onion

⅓ cup balsamic vinaigrette dressing

⅓ cup shredded or shaved Parmesan cheese

Combine lettuce, chickpeas, pepperoni, olives and onion in large bowl. Add vinaigrette; toss gently to coat. Sprinkle with cheese.

GRILLED TRI-COLORED PEPPER SALAD

makes 4 to 6 servings

1 *each* large red, yellow and green bell pepper, cut into halves or quarters

⅓ cup extra virgin olive oil

3 tablespoons balsamic vinegar

2 cloves garlic, minced

¼ teaspoon salt

¼ teaspoon black pepper

⅓ cup crumbled goat cheese

¼ cup thinly sliced fresh basil leaves

1. Prepare grill for direct cooking.

2. Grill bell peppers, skin side down, covered, over high heat 10 to 12 minutes or until skins are charred. Transfer to paper bag. Close bag; let stand 10 to 15 minutes. Remove and discard skin; rinse peppers to remove any remaining charred bits.

3. Place bell peppers in shallow serving dish. Whisk oil, vinegar, garlic, salt and black pepper in small bowl until well blended. Pour dressing over bell peppers; let stand at room temperature 30 minutes. (Or cover and refrigerate up to 24 hours. Bring to room temperature before serving.)

4. Sprinkle with goat cheese and basil just before serving.

RAVIOLI PANZANELLA SALAD

makes 4 main-dish or 6 side-dish servings

1 package (9 ounces) refrigerated fresh cheese ravioli or tortellini

2 tablespoons olive oil

2 teaspoons white wine vinegar

⅛ teaspoon black pepper

1 cup halved grape tomatoes or 1 chopped tomato

½ cup sliced pimiento-stuffed olives

¼ cup finely chopped celery

1 shallot, finely chopped *or* ¼ cup finely chopped red onion

¼ cup chopped fresh Italian parsley

1. Cook ravioli according to package directions. Drain well; transfer to large serving bowl. Let stand 10 minutes.

2. Meanwhile, whisk oil, vinegar and pepper in small bowl until well blended; pour over ravioli.

3. Add tomatoes, olives, celery and shallot; toss gently to coat. Sprinkle with parsley.

NOTE: Panzanella is a classic Italian salad that pairs a tangy vinaigrette dressing with chopped vegetables and bread cubes. It's a delicious way to use up leftover bread before it goes stale. This variation replaces the bread with ravioli.

WARM SHRIMP AND ARTICHOKE SALAD >

makes 4 servings

1 can (14 ounces) quartered artichoke hearts, drained

20 frozen cooked tail-on premium shrimp (12 ounces)

½ cup Italian vinaigrette dressing

1 package (12 ounces) mixed greens

¼ cup shredded Parmesan cheese

1. Combine artichokes, shrimp and dressing in large skillet; cover and cook over medium heat 10 minutes, stirring occasionally.

2. Divide mixed greens among four serving plates; top with shrimp mixture. Sprinkle with cheese.

PORTOBELLO AND FONTINA SANDWICHES

makes 2 sandwiches

2 teaspoons olive oil, plus additional for brushing

2 large portobello mushrooms, stems removed

Salt and black pepper

2 to 3 tablespoons sun-dried tomato pesto

4 slices crusty Italian bread

4 ounces fontina cheese, sliced

½ cup fresh basil leaves

1. Preheat broiler. Line baking sheet with foil.

2. Drizzle 2 teaspoons oil over both sides of mushrooms; season with salt and pepper. Place mushrooms, gill sides up, on prepared baking sheet. Broil 4 minutes per side or until mushrooms are tender. Cut into ¼-inch-thick slices.

3. Spread pesto evenly over two bread slices. Layer with mushrooms, cheese and basil; top with remaining bread slices. Brush outsides of sandwiches lightly with additional oil.

4. Heat large grill pan or skillet over medium heat. Add sandwiches; press down lightly with spatula or weigh down with small plate. Cook 5 minutes per side or until cheese is melted and bread is golden brown.

FENNEL, OLIVE AND RADICCHIO SALAD

makes 4 servings

½ cup Italian- or Greek-style black olives, divided

¼ cup extra virgin olive oil

1 tablespoon lemon juice

1 flat anchovy fillet *or* ½ teaspoon anchovy paste

¼ teaspoon salt

Pinch black pepper

Pinch sugar

1 bulb fennel

1 head radicchio*

*Radicchio, a tart red chicory, is available in large supermarkets and specialty food shops. If it is not available, substitute 2 heads of Belgian endive, which has a similar texture and a slightly bitter flavor.

1. Cut 3 olives in half; remove and discard pits. Combine pitted olives, oil, lemon juice and anchovy in food processor or blender; process 5 seconds. Add salt, pepper and sugar; process about 5 seconds or until olives are finely chopped. Set aside.

2. Cut off and discard fennel stalks; reserve green leafy tops (fronds) for garnish. Cut off and discard root end of bulb and any discolored parts of bulb. Cut fennel bulb lengthwise into wedges; separate each wedge into segments.

3. Separate radicchio leaves; rinse thoroughly. Drain well.

4. Arrange radicchio, fennel and remaining olives on serving plates or platter. Spoon dressing over salad; garnish with reserved fennel fronds. Serve immediately.

PANINI WITH
FRESH MOZZARELLA AND BASIL

makes 4 servings

½ cup Italian vinaigrette dressing

1 loaf (16 ounces) Italian bread, cut in half lengthwise

6 ounces fresh mozzarella cheese, cut into 12 slices

8 ounces thinly sliced oven-roasted deli turkey

½ cup thinly sliced red onion

1 large tomato, thinly sliced

12 to 16 fresh whole basil leaves

⅛ teaspoon red pepper flakes

1. Preheat indoor grill. Brush dressing evenly over both cut sides of bread.

2. Arrange cheese evenly over bottom half of bread; top with turkey, onion, tomato and basil. Sprinkle with red pepper flakes. Cover with top half of bread; press down firmly. Cut into four sandwiches.

3. Place sandwiches on grill; close lid. Cook 5 to 7 minutes or until cheese is melted and bread is golden brown.

MARINATED VEGETABLE SALAD >

makes 4 servings

½ (14-ounce) can quartered artichoke hearts, drained

6 ounces grape or cherry tomatoes, halved

½ cup chopped green bell pepper

¼ cup finely chopped red onion

2 ounces mozzarella cheese, cut into ¼-inch cubes

2 tablespoons white wine vinegar

1 tablespoon chopped fresh oregano *or* 1 teaspoon dried oregano

1 teaspoon sugar

¼ teaspoon salt

⅛ teaspoon red pepper flakes

Combine all ingredients in medium bowl; toss to coat. Serve immediately or refrigerate 1 hour to allow flavors to blend.

FRESH TOMATO AND MOZZARELLA SALAD

makes 4 servings

1 package (8 ounces) fresh mozzarella cheese

1 pound ripe tomatoes

Fresh basil leaves

1 tablespoon balsamic or red wine vinegar

¼ teaspoon Dijon mustard

Pinch *each* sugar, salt and black pepper

¼ cup extra virgin olive oil

Salt and black pepper

1. Cut cheese into ¼-inch slices. Cut tomatoes into ¼-inch slices. Arrange cheese, tomatoes and basil leaves overlapping on large plate or platter.

2. Whisk vinegar, mustard, sugar, salt and pepper in small bowl until smooth. Add oil in thin, steady stream, whisking until well blended.

3. Drizzle dressing over cheese, tomatoes and basil. Sprinkle with additional salt and pepper.

PORTOBELLO PROVOLONE PANINI

makes 4 servings

6 to 8 ounces sliced portobello mushrooms

⅓ cup plus 1 tablespoon olive oil, divided

3 tablespoons balsamic vinegar

1 clove garlic, minced

½ teaspoon salt

¼ teaspoon black pepper

1 loaf (16 ounces) ciabatta or Italian bread

8 ounces sliced provolone cheese

¼ cup chopped fresh basil

8 ounces plum tomatoes, thinly sliced

3 tablespoons whole grain Dijon mustard

1. Combine mushrooms, ⅓ cup oil, vinegar, garlic, salt and pepper in large resealable food storage bag. Seal bag; shake to coat. Let stand 15 minutes, turning frequently. (Mushrooms may be prepared up to 24 hours in advance; refrigerate and turn occasionally.)

2. Preheat indoor grill. Brush both sides of bread with remaining 1 tablespoon oil; cut bread in half lengthwise.

3. Arrange mushrooms over bottom half of bread; drizzle with some of remaining marinade. Top with cheese, basil and tomatoes. Spread mustard over cut side of remaining half of bread; place over tomatoes. Cut sandwich into four pieces.

4. Grill sandwiches 8 minutes or until cheese is melted and bread is golden brown. Wrap each sandwich tightly in foil to keep warm or serve at room temperature.

SPRINGTIME PANZANELLA

makes 4 servings

4 tablespoons extra virgin olive oil, divided

2 cloves garlic, minced, divided

4 slices bread, cut into 1-inch cubes

1 teaspoon salt, divided

1 pound asparagus, cut into 1-inch pieces

¼ cup chopped carrot

½ cup finely chopped red onion

2 tablespoons white wine vinegar

1 tablespoon lemon juice

½ teaspoon Dijon mustard

2 tablespoons shredded Parmesan cheese

1. Preheat oven to 425°F. Spray two baking sheets with nonstick cooking spray.

2. Combine 1 tablespoon oil and 1 clove garlic in large bowl. Add bread cubes; toss to coat. Spread in single layer on one baking sheet. Combine 1 tablespoon oil, remaining 1 clove garlic and ½ teaspoon salt in same bowl. Add asparagus and carrot; toss to coat. Spread on second baking sheet.

3. Bake bread cubes and vegetables 15 minutes, stirring once. Let stand 5 to 10 minutes to cool slightly.

4. Meanwhile, combine onion, vinegar, remaining 2 tablespoons oil, lemon juice, mustard and remaining ½ teaspoon salt in same large bowl; mix well. Add toasted bread cubes and vegetables; toss gently to coat. Top with cheese just before serving.

ARUGULA SALAD WITH
SUN-DRIED TOMATO VINAIGRETTE

makes 4 servings

¼ cup chopped oil-packed sun-dried tomatoes

3 tablespoons extra virgin olive oil

1½ tablespoons balsamic vinegar

¼ teaspoon salt

¼ teaspoon black pepper

1 package (5 ounces) baby arugula

1 cup halved grape tomatoes

¼ cup shaved Parmesan cheese

¼ cup pine nuts, toasted* (optional)

To toast pine nuts, cook in medium skillet over medium heat 2 minutes or until lightly browned, stirring frequently.

1. Combine sun-dried tomatoes, oil, vinegar, salt and pepper in blender or food processor; blend until smooth.

2. Combine arugula and grape tomatoes in large bowl; drizzle with dressing. Top with cheese and pine nuts, if desired.

PASTA

CLASSIC FETTUCCINE ALFREDO

makes 4 servings

12 ounces uncooked fettuccine

⅔ cup whipping cream

6 tablespoons (¾ stick) butter

½ teaspoon salt

Generous dash white pepper

Generous dash ground nutmeg

1 cup grated Parmesan cheese

2 tablespoons chopped fresh Italian parsley

1. Cook pasta according to package directions; drain. Return to saucepan; cover to keep warm.

2. Meanwhile, heat cream and butter in large heavy skillet over medium-low heat until butter melts and mixture bubbles, stirring frequently. Cook and stir 2 minutes. Stir in salt, pepper and nutmeg. Remove from heat; gradually stir in cheese until well blended and smooth. Return to low heat, if necessary; do not let sauce bubble or cheese will become lumpy and tough.

3. Pour sauce over pasta. Cook and stir over low heat 2 to 3 minutes or until sauce is thickened and pasta is evenly coated. Sprinkle with parsley. Serve immediately.

PENNE WITH RICOTTA, TOMATOES AND BASIL

makes 4 servings

1 package (16 ounces) uncooked penne pasta

2 cans (about 14 ounces each) diced Italian-seasoned tomatoes, drained

1 container (15 ounces) ricotta cheese

⅔ cup chopped fresh basil

¼ cup olive oil

1 tablespoon balsamic vinegar

1 clove garlic, minced

1 teaspoon salt

¼ teaspoon red pepper flakes or black pepper

Grated Parmesan cheese

1. Cook pasta according to package directions; drain.

2. Meanwhile, combine tomatoes, ricotta, basil, oil, vinegar, garlic, salt and red pepper flakes in large bowl; mix well.

3. Add pasta to ricotta mixture; toss gently to coat. Sprinkle with cheese. Serve immediately.

LINGUINE WITH CLAM SAUCE

makes 4 servings

8 ounces uncooked linguine

2 tablespoons olive oil

1 cup chopped onion

1 can (about 14 ounces) Italian-style stewed tomatoes, drained and chopped

2 cloves garlic, minced

2 teaspoons dried basil

½ cup dry white wine or chicken broth

1 can (10 ounces) whole baby clams, drained, juice reserved

⅓ cup chopped fresh parsley

¼ teaspoon salt

¼ teaspoon black pepper

1. Cook linguine according to package directions; drain.

2. Meanwhile, heat oil in large skillet over medium heat. Add onion; cook and stir 3 minutes or until softened. Add tomatoes, garlic and basil; cook and stir 3 minutes. Stir in wine and reserved clam juice; bring to a boil. Reduce heat to low; cook 5 minutes.

3. Stir in clams, parsley, salt and pepper; cook 1 to 2 minutes or until heated through. Spoon sauce over linguine; toss to coat. Serve immediately.

PASTA WITH BROCCOLI RABE

makes 6 servings

½ teaspoon salt

1 pound broccoli rabe,* stems trimmed

¼ cup extra virgin olive oil

2 cloves garlic, minced

½ teaspoon red pepper flakes

1 package (16 ounces) uncooked
   ziti pasta

2 tomatoes, seeded and chopped

*Broccoli rabe, also called rapini, has 6- to 9-inch stalks with clusters of tiny, broccoli-like buds. It has a stronger, slightly more bitter flavor than broccoli, which can be substituted for a milder flavor

1. Bring large saucepan of water to a boil. Add salt and broccoli rabe; cook about 5 minutes or until broccoli is crisp-tender and still bright green. Remove broccoli from saucepan to colander, leaving cooking water in saucepan. Rinse broccoli under cold running water to stop cooking; set aside.

2. Heat oil in large skillet over medium heat. Add garlic and red pepper flakes; cook and stir 1 minute or just until garlic begins to sizzle. Turn off heat.

3. Bring saucepan with broccoli cooking water to a boil. Add pasta; cook until al dente. Drain pasta, reserving 1 cup cooking water.

4. Chop broccoli into 1-inch pieces. Add broccoli to oil and garlic mixture in skillet; cook over medium heat 2 minutes or until hot. Add pasta and tomatoes; toss to blend, adding pasta water as needed.

CREAMY FETTUCCINE WITH ASPARAGUS AND LIMA BEANS

makes 4 servings

8   ounces uncooked fettuccine

2   tablespoons butter

2   cups fresh asparagus pieces
    (about 1 inch)

1   cup frozen lima beans, thawed

¼   teaspoon black pepper

½   cup vegetable broth

1   cup half-and-half or whipping
    cream

1   cup grated Parmesan cheese

1. Cook fettuccine according to package directions; drain. Return to saucepan; cover to keep warm.

2. Meanwhile, melt butter in large skillet over medium-high heat. Add asparagus, lima beans and pepper; cook and stir 3 minutes. Add broth; cook 3 minutes. Add half-and-half; cook 3 to 4 minutes or until vegetables are tender.

3. Add vegetable mixture and cheese to pasta; toss gently to coat. Serve immediately.

SPICY MANICOTTI

makes 4 to 6 servings

3 cups ricotta cheese

1 cup grated Parmesan cheese, divided

2 eggs, lightly beaten

2½ tablespoons chopped fresh parsley

1 teaspoon Italian seasoning

½ teaspoon garlic powder

½ teaspoon salt

½ teaspoon black pepper

1 pound uncooked spicy Italian sausage

1 can (28 ounces) crushed tomatoes

1 jar (26 ounces) marinara sauce

1 package (8 ounces) uncooked manicotti pasta

1. Preheat oven to 375°F. Spray 13×9-inch baking dish with nonstick cooking spray.

2. Combine ricotta, ¾ cup Parmesan, egg, parsley, Italian seasoning, garlic powder, salt and pepper in medium bowl; mix well.

3. Crumble sausage into large skillet; cook over medium-high heat until no longer pink, stirring to separate meat. Drain sausage on paper towels; drain fat from skillet. Add tomatoes and marinara sauce to skillet; bring to a boil over high heat. Reduce heat to low; cook 10 minutes, stirring occasionally. Pour about one third of sauce into prepared baking dish.

4. Stuff each shell with about ½ cup ricotta mixture. Place filled shells in prepared baking dish; top with sausage and remaining sauce. Cover with foil.

5. Bake 50 minutes to 1 hour or until pasta is tender. Let stand 5 minutes before serving. Sprinkle with remaining ¼ cup Parmesan.

PASTA WITH ONIONS AND GOAT CHEESE

makes 4 to 6 servings

1 tablespoon olive oil

3 to 4 cups thinly sliced sweet onions

8 ounces uncooked campanelle or farfalle pasta

¾ cup (3 ounces) crumbled goat cheese

¼ cup milk

1 clove garlic, minced

2 tablespoons dry white wine or vegetable broth

1½ teaspoons chopped fresh sage *or ½ teaspoon dried sage*

½ teaspoon salt

¼ teaspoon black pepper

¼ cup chopped toasted walnuts

1. Heat oil in large nonstick skillet over medium heat. Add onions; cook about 20 to 25 minutes or until golden brown, stirring occasionally.

2. Meanwhile, cook pasta according to package directions. Combine goat cheese and milk in small bowl; stir until well blended and smooth.

3. Add garlic to onions in skillet; cook about 3 minutes or until softened. Add wine, sage, salt and pepper; cook until liquid has evaporated. Remove from heat.

4. Drain pasta; add to skillet with goat cheese mixture. Stir until cheese is melted. Sprinkle with walnuts.

PESTO WITH LINGUINE

makes 4 servings (about ¾ cup pesto sauce)

12 ounces uncooked linguine

2 tablespoons butter

¼ cup plus 1 tablespoon extra virgin olive oil, divided

2 tablespoons pine nuts

1 cup tightly packed fresh basil leaves

2 cloves garlic

¼ teaspoon salt

¼ cup grated Parmesan cheese

1½ tablespoons grated Romano cheese

1. Cook linguine according to package directions; drain. Toss with butter in large serving bowl; set aside and keep warm.

2. Meanwhile, heat 1 tablespoon oil in small skillet over medium-low heat. Add pine nuts; cook and stir 30 to 45 seconds until lightly browned, shaking skillet constantly. Remove to food processor or blender with slotted spoon.

3. Add basil, garlic and salt to food processor. With motor running, add remaining ¼ cup oil in slow, steady stream; process until well blended and pine nuts are finely chopped. Transfer to small bowl; stir in Parmesan and Romano.*

4. Add pesto sauce to pasta; toss well to coat. Serve immediately.

*Pesto can be stored at this point in airtight container. Pour thin layer of olive oil over pesto; cover and refrigerate up to 1 week. Bring to room temperature before using. Proceed as directed in step 4.

SLOW COOKER STUFFED SHELLS

makes 4 to 6 servings

1 package (16 ounces) uncooked
    jumbo pasta shells

1 container (15 ounces) ricotta cheese

7 ounces frozen chopped spinach,
    thawed and squeezed dry

½ cup grated Parmesan cheese

1 egg, lightly beaten

1 clove garlic, minced

½ teaspoon salt

1 jar (24 ounces) marinara sauce

½ cup (2 ounces) shredded mozzarella
    cheese

2 teaspoons olive oil

SLOW COOKER DIRECTIONS

1. Cook pasta shells according to package directions; drain. Combine ricotta, spinach, Parmesan, egg, garlic and salt in large bowl; mix well.

2. Spoon 2 to 3 tablespoons ricotta mixture into each pasta shell. Pour ¼ cup marinara sauce in bottom of slow cooker; top with enough filled pasta shells to cover bottom of slow cooker. Top with ¼ cup marinara sauce; cover with remaining pasta shells. Top with any remaining marinara sauce; sprinkle with mozzarella. Drizzle with oil.

3. Cover; cook on HIGH 3 to 4 hours or until mozzarella is melted and sauce is hot and bubbly.

PASTA CAMPAGNOLO

makes 4 servings

3 tablespoons olive oil

8 ounces Italian sausage, casings removed

1 small onion, finely chopped

1 red bell pepper, cut into ¼-inch strips

2 cloves garlic, minced

⅓ cup dry white wine

1 can (28 ounces) crushed tomatoes

1 can (8 ounces) tomato sauce

4 tablespoons chopped fresh basil, divided, plus additional for garnish

½ teaspoon salt

¼ teaspoon black pepper

⅛ teaspoon red pepper flakes

1 package (16 ounces) uncooked rigatoni or penne pasta

¼ cup grated Romano cheese

1 package (4 ounces) goat cheese, cut crosswise into 8 slices

1. Heat oil in large saucepan over medium heat. Break sausage into ½-inch pieces; add to saucepan. Cook about 5 minutes or until browned, stirring occasionally. Add onion and bell pepper; cook and stir 4 minutes or until vegetables are softened. Add garlic; cook and stir 1 minute.

2. Stir in wine; cook about 5 minutes or until most of liquid has evaporated. Stir in tomatoes, tomato sauce, 2 tablespoons basil, salt, black pepper and red pepper flakes; bring to a boil. Reduce heat to medium-low; cook 20 minutes or until sauce has thickened slightly.

3. Meanwhile, cook pasta in boiling salted water according to package directions. Add hot cooked pasta, Romano cheese and remaining 2 tablespoons basil to sauce; stir gently to coat. Cook just until heated through.

4. Top each serving with 1 or 2 slices of goat cheese; garnish with additional basil.

ANGEL HAIR PASTA WITH SEAFOOD SAUCE

makes 6 servings

8 ounces uncooked angel hair pasta

1 tablespoon olive oil

½ cup chopped onion

2 cloves garlic, minced

3 pounds plum tomatoes, seeded and chopped

¼ cup chopped fresh basil

2 tablespoons chopped fresh oregano

1 teaspoon red pepper flakes

½ teaspoon sugar

2 bay leaves

8 ounces firm whitefish, such as sea bass, monkfish or grouper, cut into ¾-inch pieces

8 ounces bay scallops or shucked oysters

2 tablespoons chopped fresh Italian parsley

1. Cook pasta according to package directions; drain.

2. Meanwhile, heat oil in large nonstick skillet over medium heat. Add onion and garlic; cook and stir 3 minutes or until onion is translucent. Add tomatoes, basil, oregano, red pepper flakes, sugar and bay leaves; cook over low heat 15 minutes, stirring occasionally.

3. Add whitefish and scallops; cook 3 to 4 minutes or until fish begins to flake when tested with fork and scallops are opaque. Remove and discard bay leaves.

4. Combine pasta and seafood sauce in large bowl; toss gently to coat. Sprinkle with parsley.

VEGETABLE PENNE ITALIANO

makes 4 servings

1 tablespoon olive oil

1 red bell pepper, cut into ½-inch pieces

1 green bell pepper, cut into ½-inch pieces

1 medium sweet onion, halved and thinly sliced

3 cloves garlic, minced

2 tablespoons tomato paste

2 teaspoons salt

1 teaspoon sugar

1 teaspoon Italian seasoning

¼ teaspoon black pepper

1 can (28 ounces) Italian plum tomatoes, undrained, chopped

8 ounces uncooked penne pasta

Grated Parmesan cheese

Chopped fresh basil

1. Heat oil in large skillet over medium-high heat. Add bell peppers, onion and garlic; cook and stir 8 minutes or until vegetables are crisp-tender.

2. Add tomato paste, salt, sugar, Italian seasoning and black pepper; cook and stir 1 minute. Stir in tomatoes with liquid. Reduce heat to medium-low; cook 15 minutes or until vegetables are tender and sauce is thickened.

3. Meanwhile, cook pasta in large saucepan of salted water according to package directions; drain and return to saucepan. Add sauce; stir gently to coat. Divide among serving bowls; top with cheese and basil.

CLASSIC LASAGNA

makes about 8 servings

1 tablespoon olive oil

8 ounces bulk mild Italian sausage

8 ounces ground beef

1 medium onion, chopped

3 cloves garlic, minced, divided

1½ teaspoons salt, divided

1 can (28 ounces) crushed tomatoes

1 can (28 ounces) diced tomatoes

2 teaspoons Italian seasoning

1 egg

1 container (15 ounces) ricotta cheese

¾ cup grated Parmesan cheese, divided

½ cup minced fresh parsley

¼ teaspoon black pepper

12 uncooked no-boil lasagna noodles

4 cups (16 ounces) shredded mozzarella

1. Preheat oven to 350°F. Spray 13×9-inch baking dish with nonstick cooking spray.

2. Heat oil in large saucepan over medium-high heat. Add sausage, beef, onion, 2 cloves garlic and 1 teaspoon salt; cook and stir 10 minutes or until meat is no longer pink, breaking up meat with wooden spoon. Add crushed tomatoes, diced tomatoes and Italian seasoning; bring to a boil. Reduce heat to medium-low; cook 15 minutes, stirring occasionally.

3. Meanwhile, beat egg in medium bowl. Stir in ricotta, ½ cup Parmesan, parsley, remaining 1 clove garlic, ½ teaspoon salt and pepper until well blended.

4. Spread ¼ cup sauce in prepared baking dish. Top with 3 noodles, breaking to fit if necessary. Spread one third of ricotta mixture over noodles. Sprinkle with 1 cup mozzarella; top with 2 cups sauce. Repeat layers of noodles, ricotta mixture, mozzarella and sauce two times. Top with remaining 3 noodles, sauce, 1 cup mozzarella and ¼ cup Parmesan. Cover dish with foil sprayed with cooking spray.

5. Bake 30 minutes. Remove foil; bake 10 to 15 minutes or until hot and bubbly. Let stand 10 minutes before serving.

LINGUINE WITH HERBS, TOMATOES AND CAPERS

makes 4 servings

1 package (9 ounces) refrigerated fresh linguine

2 tablespoons olive oil

2 cloves garlic, minced

2 cups chopped tomatoes

¼ cup finely chopped green onions

3 tablespoons capers, drained

2 tablespoons finely chopped fresh basil

¼ teaspoon salt

⅛ teaspoon black pepper

½ cup shredded Parmesan cheese

1. Cook linguine according to package directions; drain.

2. Meanwhile, heat oil in large skillet over medium-high heat. Add garlic and tomatoes; cook 3 minutes or until tomatoes begin to soften, stirring frequently. Stir in green onions, capers and basil. Season with salt and pepper.

3. Add linguine to skillet; toss gently to coat. Sprinkle with cheese.

PESTO CAVATAPPI

makes 4 to 6 servings

PESTO

- 2 **cups packed fresh basil leaves***
- 1 **cup walnuts, toasted**
- ½ **cup shredded Parmesan cheese, plus additional for serving**
- 4 **cloves garlic**
- 1 **teaspoon salt**
- ¼ **teaspoon black pepper**
- ¾ **cup extra virgin olive oil**

PASTA

- 1 **package (16 ounces) uncooked cavatappi pasta**
- 1 **tablespoon extra virgin olive oil**
- 2 **plum tomatoes, diced (1½ cups)**
- 1 **package (8 ounces) sliced mushrooms**
- ¼ **cup dry white wine**
- ¼ **cup vegetable broth**
- ¼ **cup whipping cream**

*Or substitute 1 cup packed fresh parsley leaves for half of basil.

1. For pesto, combine basil, walnuts, ½ cup cheese, garlic, salt and black pepper in food processor; pulse until coarsely chopped. With motor running, add ¾ cup oil in thin, steady stream; process until well blended. Measure 1 cup pesto for pasta; reserve remaining pesto for another use.

2. Cook pasta in large saucepan of boiling salted water according to package directions; drain. Return to saucepan; cover to keep warm.

3. Meanwhile, heat 1 tablespoon oil in large skillet over medium-high heat. Add tomatoes and mushrooms; cook about 7 minutes or until most of liquid has evaporated, stirring occasionally. Add wine, broth and cream; bring to a boil. Reduce heat to low; cook about 4 minutes or until sauce thickens slightly. Stir in 1 cup pesto; cook just until heated through.

4. Pour sauce over pasta; stir gently to coat. Serve with additional cheese.

FETTUCCINE ALLA CARBONARA

makes 4 servings

12 ounces uncooked fettuccine

4 ounces pancetta or bacon, cut
    crosswise into ½-inch pieces

3 cloves garlic, cut into halves

¼ cup dry white wine

⅓ cup whipping cream

1 egg

1 egg yolk

⅔ cup grated Parmesan cheese,
   divided

Dash white pepper

1. Cook fettuccine according to package directions; drain. Return to saucepan; cover to keep warm.

2. Combine pancetta and garlic in large skillet; cook and stir over medium-low heat 4 minutes or until lightly browned. Drain but 2 tablespoons drippings from skillet. Add wine to skillet; cook over medium heat 3 minutes or until almost evaporated. Add cream; cook and stir 2 minutes. Remove from heat; discard garlic.

3. Whisk egg and egg yolk in top of double boiler; place over simmering water, adjusting heat to maintain simmer. Whisk ⅓ cup cheese and pepper into egg mixture; cook and stir until thickened.

4. Pour pancetta mixture over fettuccine; toss to coat. Cook over medium-low heat until heated through. Add egg mixture; toss to coat. Serve with remaining ⅓ cup cheese.

MAIN DISHES

SHRIMP SCAMPI

makes 4 servings

3 tablespoons butter

2 tablespoons minced garlic

1½ pounds large raw shrimp, peeled and deveined (with tails on)

6 green onions, thinly sliced

¼ cup dry white wine

2 tablespoons lemon juice

Chopped fresh Italian parsley

Salt and black pepper

Lemon wedges (optional)

1. Heat butter in large skillet over medium heat. Add garlic; cook and stir 1 to 2 minutes or until softened but not brown. Add shrimp, green onions, wine and lemon juice; cook 2 to 4 minutes or until shrimp are pink and opaque, stirring occasionally.

2. Sprinkle with parsley; season with salt and pepper. Serve with lemon wedges, if desired.

PORK MEDALLIONS WITH MARSALA

makes 4 servings

¼ cup all-purpose flour

½ teaspoon salt

⅛ teaspoon black pepper

1 pound pork tenderloin, cut into ½-inch slices

2 tablespoons olive oil

1 shallot, finely chopped

1 clove garlic, minced

½ cup sweet Marsala wine

2 tablespoons chopped fresh parsley

1. Combine flour, salt and pepper in shallow dish. Coat pork lightly with flour mixture; shake off excess.

2. Heat oil in large skillet over medium-high heat. Add pork; cook 3 minutes per side or until browned. Remove to plate.

3. Add shallot and garlic to skillet; cook and stir over medium heat 1 minute. Add wine and pork; cook 3 minutes or until pork is barely pink in center, turning once. Remove pork to clean plate. Add parsley to skillet; cook 2 to 3 minutes or until sauce thickens slightly. Serve sauce over pork.

CHICKEN SCARPIELLO

makes 6 servings

3 tablespoons extra virgin olive oil, divided

1 pound spicy Italian sausage, cut into 1-inch pieces

1 whole chicken (about 3 pounds), cut into 10 pieces*

1 teaspoon salt, divided

1 large onion, chopped

2 red, yellow or orange bell peppers, cut into ¼-inch strips

3 cloves garlic, minced

½ cup dry white wine (such as sauvignon blanc)

½ cup chicken broth

½ cup coarsely chopped seeded hot cherry peppers

½ cup liquid from cherry pepper jar

1 teaspoon dried oregano

Additional salt and black pepper

¼ cup chopped fresh Italian parsley

Or, purchase 2 bone-in chicken leg quarters and 2 chicken breasts; separate drumsticks and thighs and cut breasts in half.

1. Heat 1 tablespoon oil in large skillet over medium-high heat. Add sausage; cook about 10 minutes or until well browned on all sides, stirring occasionally. Remove sausage to plate.

2. Heat 1 tablespoon oil in same skillet. Sprinkle chicken with ½ teaspoon salt; arrange skin side down in single layer in skillet (cook in batches, if necessary). Cook about 6 minutes per side or until browned. Remove to plate. Drain oil from skillet.

3. Heat remaining 1 tablespoon oil in skillet. Add onion and ½ teaspoon salt; cook and stir 2 minutes or until onion is softened, scraping up browned bits from bottom of skillet. Add bell peppers and garlic; cook and stir 5 minutes. Stir in wine; cook until liquid is reduced by half. Stir in broth, cherry peppers, cherry pepper liquid and oregano. Season with additional salt and black pepper; bring to a simmer.

4. Return sausage and chicken along with any accumulated juices to skillet. Partially cover skillet; cook 10 minutes. Uncover; cook 15 minutes or until chicken is cooked through (165°F). Sprinkle with parsley.

TIP: If too much liquid remains in the skillet when the chicken is cooked through, remove the chicken and sausage and continue simmering the sauce to reduce it slightly.

GRILLED SWORDFISH SICILIAN STYLE

makes 4 to 6 servings

3 tablespoons extra virgin olive oil

1 clove garlic, minced

2 tablespoons lemon juice

¾ teaspoon salt

⅛ teaspoon black pepper

3 tablespoons capers, drained

1 tablespoon chopped fresh oregano or basil

1½ pounds swordfish steaks (¾ inch thick)

1. Prepare grill for direct cooking. Oil grid.

2. Heat oil in small saucepan over low heat. Add garlic; cook and stir 1 minute. Remove from heat; cool slightly. Whisk in lemon juice, salt and pepper until salt is dissolved. Stir in capers and oregano.

3. Grill fish over medium heat 7 to 8 minutes or until center is opaque, turning once. Serve with sauce.

BRAISED SHORT RIBS IN RED WINE

makes 4 to 6 servings

3 pounds beef short ribs, trimmed

Salt and black pepper

1 to 2 tablespoons vegetable oil

2 large onions, sliced

2 packages (8 ounces each) baby bella or cremini mushrooms, quartered

2 cups dry red wine

2 cups beef broth

2 cloves garlic, minced

2 teaspoons Italian seasoning

Mashed potatoes or polenta (optional)

SLOW COOKER DIRECTIONS

1. Spray slow cooker with nonstick cooking spray. Season short ribs with salt and pepper. Heat 1 tablespoon oil in large skillet over medium-high heat. Brown short ribs on all sides, working in batches and adding additional oil as needed. Remove to slow cooker.

2. Add onions to skillet; cook and stir 5 minutes or until translucent. Stir in mushrooms, wine, broth, garlic and Italian seasoning; bring to a simmer. Cook 3 minutes, stirring occasionally. Pour over short ribs in slow cooker.

3. Cover; cook on LOW 10 to 12 hours or on HIGH 6 to 8 hours or until meat is tender. Season with additional salt and pepper. Remove short ribs and vegetables to serving plate.

4. Strain cooking liquid; serve over short ribs and potatoes, if desired.

SAUSAGE AND POLENTA CASSEROLE

makes 4 servings

1 **tablespoon olive oil**	1 **pound bulk Italian sausage**
1 **cup chopped mushrooms**	1 **jar (24 ounces) meatless pasta sauce**
1 **red bell pepper, diced**	1 **roll (16 to 18 ounces) polenta**
1 **onion, diced**	¼ **cup shredded Parmesan cheese**

1. Preheat oven to 350°F. Spray 8-inch square baking dish with nonstick cooking spray.

2. Heat oil in large skillet over medium heat. Add mushrooms, bell pepper and onion; cook and stir 5 minutes or until vegetables are tender. Add sausage; cook until sausage is browned, stirring to break up meat. Drain fat. Add pasta sauce; cook 5 minutes, stirring occasionally.

3. Cut polenta crosswise into nine slices; arrange in prepared baking dish. Top with sausage mixture.

4. Bake 15 minutes or until heated through. Sprinkle with cheese.

TUNA STEAKS WITH TOMATOES AND OLIVES

makes 4 servings

2 tablespoons olive oil, divided

1 onion, quartered and sliced

1 clove garlic, minced

1⅓ cups chopped tomatoes

¼ cup sliced pitted black olives

2 anchovy fillets, finely chopped (optional)

2 tablespoons chopped fresh basil

½ teaspoon salt, divided

⅛ teaspoon red pepper flakes

4 tuna steaks (¾ inch thick)

Black pepper

¼ cup toasted pine nuts*

To toast pine nuts, cook in small skillet over medium heat 2 minutes or until lightly browned, stirring frequently.

1. Heat 1 tablespoon oil in large skillet over medium heat. Add onion; cook and stir 4 minutes. Add garlic; cook and stir 30 seconds. Add tomatoes; cook 3 minutes, stirring occasionally. Stir in olives, anchovies, if desired, basil, ¼ teaspoon salt and red pepper flakes; cook until most of liquid has evaporated.

2. Meanwhile, sprinkle fish with remaining ¼ teaspoon salt and black pepper, if desired. Heat remaining 1 tablespoon oil in large nonstick skillet over medium-high heat. Add fish; cook 2 minutes per side or until medium rare. Serve with tomato mixture; sprinkle with pine nuts.

BEEF SPIEDINI WITH ORZO

makes 4 servings

1½ pounds beef top sirloin steak,
    cut into 1×1¼-inch pieces

¼ cup olive oil

¼ cup dry red wine

2 cloves garlic, minced

1 teaspoon dried rosemary

1 teaspoon salt, divided

½ teaspoon dried thyme

½ teaspoon coarsely ground black
    pepper

6 cups water

1 cup uncooked orzo

1 tablespoon butter

1 tablespoon chopped fresh parsley

   Fresh rosemary sprigs (optional)

1. Place beef in large resealable food storage bag. Combine oil, wine, garlic, dried rosemary, ½ teaspoon salt, thyme and pepper in small bowl; pour over beef. Seal bag; turn to coat. Marinate in refrigerator 15 to 30 minutes.

2. Prepare grill for direct cooking. Soak eight 6- to 8-inch wooden skewers in water 30 minutes.

3. Bring 6 cups water and remaining ½ teaspoon salt to a boil in small saucepan over high heat. Stir in orzo. Reduce heat to low; cook 15 minutes or until tender. Drain orzo; return to saucepan. Stir in butter and parsley; cover to keep warm.

4. Thread beef onto skewers. Grill skewers over medium-high heat 8 to 10 minutes, turning occasionally. Serve with orzo. Garnish skewers with fresh rosemary.

TIP: Rosemary skewers infuse the wonderful scent of rosemary into grilled foods. To make rosemary skewers, find large heavy sprigs and remove the leaves from the bottom three quarters of the sprigs. Then thread small pieces of meat on each sprig before grilling.

TUSCAN LAMB SKILLET

makes 4 servings

8 lamb rib chops (1½ pounds), cut 1 inch thick

1 tablespoon olive oil

3 teaspoons minced garlic

1 can (19 ounces) cannellini beans, rinsed and drained

1 can (about 14 ounces) Italian-style whole tomatoes, undrained, crushed with hands or coarsely chopped

1 tablespoon balsamic vinegar

2 teaspoons minced fresh rosemary

Additional fresh rosemary sprigs (optional)

1. Trim fat from lamb chops. Heat oil in large skillet over medium heat. Add lamb; cook about 4 minutes per side or until 160°F for medium doneness. Remove to plate; keep warm.

2. Add garlic to drippings in skillet; cook and stir 1 minute. Stir in beans, tomatoes with liquid, vinegar and minced rosemary; bring to a boil. Reduce heat to medium-low; cook 5 minutes.

3. Divide bean mixture among four plates; top with lamb. Garnish with additional rosemary.

ROSEMARY-GARLIC SCALLOPS WITH POLENTA

makes 2 servings

1 tablespoon olive oil

1 medium red bell pepper, cut into strips

⅓ cup chopped red onion

3 cloves garlic, minced

8 ounces fresh bay scallops

2 teaspoons chopped fresh rosemary *or* ¾ teaspoon dried rosemary

¼ teaspoon black pepper

1¼ cups chicken broth

½ cup cornmeal

¼ teaspoon salt

1. Heat oil in large nonstick skillet over medium heat. Add bell pepper, onion and garlic; cook and stir 5 minutes. Add scallops, rosemary and black pepper; cook 3 to 5 minutes or until scallops are opaque, stirring occasionally.

2. Meanwhile, combine broth, cornmeal and salt in small saucepan; bring to a boil over high heat. Reduce heat to low; cook 5 minutes or until polenta is very thick, stirring frequently. Transfer to two serving plates; top with scallop mixture.

TIP: There are two common varieties of scallops: bay and sea. Bay scallops are smaller and usually average about 100 per pound. Sea scallops are much larger, averaging about 30 per pound. If bay scallops are not available, you can substitute sea scallops; cut them into halves or thirds.

POLLO DIAVOLO (DEVILED CHICKEN)

makes 4 servings

8 bone-in chicken thighs (2½ to 3 pounds), skin removed

¼ cup olive oil

3 tablespoons lemon juice

6 cloves garlic, minced

1 teaspoon red pepper flakes

3 tablespoons butter, softened

1 teaspoon dried sage

1 teaspoon dried thyme

¾ teaspoon coarse salt

¼ teaspoon ground red pepper or black pepper

Lemon wedges

1. Place chicken in large resealable food storage bag. Combine oil, lemon juice, garlic and red pepper flakes in small bowl; pour over chicken. Seal bag; turn to coat. Refrigerate at least 1 hour or up to 8 hours, turning once.

2. Prepare grill for direct cooking. Drain chicken; reserve marinade. Place chicken on grid; brush with reserved marinade. Grill, covered, over medium-high heat 8 minutes. Turn chicken; brush with remaining marinade. Grill, covered, 8 to 10 minutes or until cooked through (165°F).

3. Meanwhile, combine butter, sage, thyme, salt and ground red pepper in small bowl; mix well. Transfer chicken to serving platter; spread herb butter over chicken. Serve with lemon wedges.

SAUSAGE, PEPPER AND ONION PIZZA

makes 4 servings

½ cup tomato sauce

1 clove garlic, minced

½ teaspoon dried basil

½ teaspoon dried oregano

⅛ teaspoon red pepper flakes (optional)

2 grilled or smoked sausage links

1 grilled red onion

1 grilled or roasted bell pepper

1 (12-inch) prepared pizza crust

1½ cups (6 ounces) shredded fontina cheese or pizza cheese blend

½ cup grated Parmesan cheese

1. Preheat oven to 450°F. Combine tomato sauce, garlic, basil, oregano and red pepper flakes, if desired, in small bowl. Cut sausages in half lengthwise, then cut crosswise into ½-inch slices. Cut onion and bell pepper into 1-inch pieces.

2. Place pizza crust on baking sheet or pizza pan. Spread tomato sauce mixture over crust to within 1 inch of edge. Sprinkle with fontina; top with sausage, onion and bell pepper. Sprinkle with Parmesan.

3. Bake 12 minutes or until crust is crisp and cheeses are melted.

TIP: To save time, substitute ½ cup pizza sauce for the tomato sauce and seasonings.

MUSHROOM RAGOÛT WITH POLENTA

makes 4 servings

1 package (about ½ ounce) dried porcini mushrooms

½ cup boiling water

1 can (about 14 ounces) vegetable broth

½ cup yellow cornmeal

1 tablespoon olive oil

⅓ cup sliced shallots or chopped onion

1 package (4 ounces) sliced mixed fresh exotic mushrooms or sliced cremini (brown) mushrooms

4 cloves garlic, minced

1 can (about 14 ounces) Italian-style diced tomatoes

¼ teaspoon red pepper flakes

¼ cup chopped fresh basil or parsley

½ cup grated Parmesan cheese

1. Place porcini mushrooms in small bowl; cover with boiling water. Let stand 10 minutes.

2. Meanwhile, whisk broth and cornmeal in large microwavable bowl. Cover with waxed paper; microwave on HIGH 5 minutes. Whisk well; microwave on HIGH 3 to 4 minutes or until polenta is very thick. Whisk again; cover and set aside.

3. Heat oil in large nonstick skillet over medium-high heat. Add shallots; cook and stir 3 minutes. Add fresh mushrooms and garlic; cook and stir 3 to 4 minutes. Stir in tomatoes and red pepper flakes.

4. Drain porcini mushrooms, reserving liquid. Strain liquid and add to skillet. If mushrooms are large, cut into ½-inch pieces; add to skillet. Bring to a boil over high heat. Reduce heat to low; cook 5 minutes or until slightly thickened, stirring occasionally. Stir in basil. Serve ragoût over polenta; sprinkle with cheese.

PORK CHOPS WITH VINEGAR PEPPERS

makes 4 servings

4 pork rib chops (about 1 inch thick)

½ teaspoon salt

¼ teaspoon black pepper

2 tablespoons olive oil

1½ cups sliced seeded hot cherry peppers (½-inch slices*)

2 cloves garlic, minced

¼ cup liquid from cherry pepper jar

¼ cup water

1 sprig fresh rosemary

Chopped fresh Italian parsley (optional)

Hot cherry peppers are also available presliced in rings.

1. Pat pork chops dry with paper towels. Season both sides with salt and black pepper.

2. Heat oil in large saucepan over medium-high heat. Add pork; cook about 5 minutes per side or until browned. Remove to plate; tent with foil.

3. Add cherry peppers and garlic to skillet; cook 2 minutes over medium heat, scraping up browned bits from bottom of skillet. Stir in cherry pepper liquid, water and rosemary.

4. Return pork along with any accumulated juices to skillet; cover and cook about 6 minutes or until pork is barely pink in center. Sprinkle with parsley, if desired.

EGGPLANT PARMESAN

makes 4 servings

1 medium eggplant (about 1 pound)

⅓ cup all-purpose flour

¼ teaspoon salt

¼ teaspoon black pepper

⅔ cup milk

1 egg

1 cup Italian-seasoned dry bread crumbs

4 to 5 tablespoons olive oil, divided

2 cups marinara sauce, heated

1 cup (4 ounces) shredded mozzarella cheese

Chopped fresh parsley (optional)

1. Preheat broiler. Spray 13×9-inch baking dish with nonstick cooking spray. Cut eggplant crosswise into ¼-inch slices. Combine flour, salt and black pepper in shallow dish. Beat milk and egg in another shallow dish. Place bread crumbs in third shallow dish.

2. Coat both sides of eggplant slices with flour mixture, shaking off excess. Dip in egg mixture, letting excess drip back into dish. Roll in bread crumbs to coat.

3. Heat 3 tablespoons oil in large skillet over medium-high heat. Working in batches, add eggplant slices to skillet in single layer; cook 3 to 4 minutes per side or until golden brown, adding additional oil as needed. Remove to paper towel-lined plate; cover loosely with foil to keep warm.

4. Arrange eggplant slices overlapping in baking dish; top with warm marinara sauce. Sprinkle with cheese.

5. Broil 2 to 3 minutes or just until cheese is melted and beginning to brown. Garnish with parsley.

ITALIAN MEAT LOAF

makes 8 servings

1 can (8 ounces) tomato sauce, divided

1 egg, lightly beaten

½ cup chopped onion

½ cup chopped green bell pepper

⅓ cup seasoned dry bread crumbs

2 tablespoons grated Parmesan cheese

½ teaspoon garlic powder

¼ teaspoon black pepper

1 pound ground beef

½ pound ground pork

1 cup (4 ounces) shredded Asiago cheese

SLOW COOKER DIRECTIONS

1. Reserve ⅓ cup tomato sauce; refrigerate until needed. Combine remaining tomato sauce and egg in large bowl. Add onion, bell pepper, bread crumbs, Parmesan, garlic powder and black pepper; stir until blended. Add ground beef and pork; mix well. Shape mixture into loaf. Carefully transfer to slow cooker.

2. Cover; cook on LOW 8 to 10 hours or on HIGH 4 to 6 hours (internal temperature should reach 170°F).

3. Spread meat loaf with reserved tomato sauce; sprinkle with Asiago. Cover; cook on HIGH 15 minutes or until cheese is melted.

CHICKEN MARSALA

makes 4 servings

4 boneless skinless chicken breasts (6 to 8 ounces each)

½ cup all-purpose flour

1 teaspoon coarse salt

¼ teaspoon black pepper

2 tablespoons olive oil

3 tablespoons butter, divided

2 cups (16 ounces) sliced mushrooms

1 shallot, minced (about 2 tablespoons)

1 clove garlic, minced

1 cup dry Marsala wine

½ cup chicken broth

Finely chopped fresh parsley

1. Pound chicken to ¼-inch thickness between two sheets of plastic wrap. Combine flour, salt and pepper in shallow dish; mix well. Coat both sides of chicken with flour mixture, shaking off excess.

2. Heat oil and 1 tablespoon butter in large skillet over medium-high heat. Add chicken in single layer; cook about 4 minutes per side or until golden brown. Remove to plate; tent with foil.

3. Add 1 tablespoon butter, mushrooms and shallot to skillet; cook about 10 minutes or until mushrooms are deep golden brown, stirring occasionally. Add garlic; cook and stir 1 minute. Stir in wine and broth; cook 2 minutes, scraping up browned bits from bottom of skillet. Stir in remaining 1 tablespoon butter until melted.

4. Return chicken to skillet; turn to coat with sauce. Cook 2 minutes or until heated through. Sprinkle with parsley.

PROSCIUTTO-WRAPPED SNAPPER

makes 4 servings

1 tablespoon plus 1 teaspoon olive oil, divided

2 cloves garlic, minced

4 skinless red snapper or halibut fillets (6 to 7 ounces each)

½ teaspoon salt

½ teaspoon black pepper

8 large fresh sage leaves

8 thin slices prosciutto (4 ounces)

¼ cup dry Marsala wine

1. Preheat oven to 400°F.

2. Combine 1 tablespoon oil and garlic in small bowl; brush over fish. Sprinkle with salt and pepper. Lay 2 sage leaves on each fillet. Wrap 2 slices prosciutto around fish to enclose sage leaves; tuck in ends of prosciutto.

3. Heat remaining 1 teaspoon oil in large ovenproof nonstick skillet over medium-high heat. Add fish, sage side down; cook 3 to 4 minutes or until prosciutto is crisp. Carefully turn fish; transfer skillet to oven.

4. Bake 8 to 10 minutes or until fish is opaque in center. Remove fish to serving plates; keep warm. Pour wine into skillet; cook over medium-high heat 2 to 3 minutes or until reduced by half, scraping up browned bits from bottom of skillet. Drizzle sauce over fish.

STEAK AL FORNO

makes 2 to 3 servings

4 cloves garlic, minced

1 tablespoon olive oil

1 tablespoon coarse salt

1 teaspoon black pepper

2 porterhouse or T-bone steaks (1 to 1¼ inches thick)

¼ cup grated Parmesan cheese (optional)

1. Prepare grill for direct cooking. Combine garlic, oil, salt and pepper in small bowl; press into both sides of steaks. Let stand 15 minutes.

2. Grill steaks, covered, over medium-high heat 7 to 10 minutes per side for medium rare (145°F) or to desired doneness. Transfer to cutting board; tent with foil. Let stand 5 minutes before slicing.

3. To serve, cut meat away from each side of bone. Cut boneless pieces into slices. Sprinkle with cheese, if desired. Serve immediately.

TIP: For a smokier flavor, soak 2 cups hickory or oak wood chips in cold water to cover for at least 30 minutes. Drain and scatter over hot coals before grilling.

SIDE DISHES

FOCACCIA

makes 12 servings

1 package (¼ ounce) active dry yeast

1 teaspoon sugar

1½ cups warm water (105° to 110°F)

4 cups all-purpose flour, divided

7 tablespoons olive oil, divided

1 teaspoon salt

¼ cup bottled roasted red peppers, drained and cut into strips

¼ cup pitted black olives

1. To proof yeast, sprinkle yeast and sugar over warm water in large bowl; stir until dissolved. Let stand 5 minutes or until bubbly. Add 3½ cups flour, 3 tablespoons oil and salt; stir until soft dough forms.

2. Turn out dough onto lightly floured surface. Knead 5 minutes or until smooth and elastic, gradually adding remaining flour to prevent sticking, if necessary. Shape dough into a ball. Place in large greased bowl; turn to grease top. Cover and let rise in warm place 1 hour or until doubled in size.

3. Brush 15×10-inch jelly-roll pan with 1 tablespoon oil. Punch down dough. Turn out dough onto lightly floured surface. Flatten dough into rectangle; roll out almost to size of pan. Transfer dough to pan; gently press to edges of pan. Poke surface of dough with end of wooden spoon handle, making indentations every 1 or 2 inches. Brush with remaining 3 tablespoons oil. Gently press roasted peppers and olives into dough. Cover and let rise in warm place 30 minutes or until doubled in size. Preheat oven to 450°F.

4. Bake 12 to 18 minutes or until golden brown. Cut into squares or rectangles. Serve warm.

PEASANT RISOTTO

makes 4 servings

1 tablespoon olive oil

3 ounces chopped prosciutto or ham

2 cloves garlic, minced

1 can (about 15 ounces) Great Northern beans, rinsed and drained

1 cup uncooked arborio rice

¼ cup chopped green onions

½ teaspoon dried sage

2 cans (about 14 ounces each) chicken broth, warmed

1½ cups packed Swiss chard, rinsed, stemmed and shredded

½ cup grated Parmesan cheese

1. Heat oil in large saucepan over medium heat. Add prosciutto and garlic; cook and stir 2 minutes until garlic is lightly browned.

2. Add beans, rice, green onions and sage; cook and stir 2 minutes. Add warm broth, ½ cup at a time, stirring frequently until broth is absorbed before adding next ½ cup. Continue until rice is tender and mixture is creamy (about 25 minutes).

3. Stir in Swiss chard and cheese. Remove from heat; cover and let stand 2 minutes or until Swiss chard is wilted. Serve immediately.

SAVORY STUFFED TOMATOES

makes 4 servings

2 large ripe tomatoes (1 to 1¼ pounds total)

¾ cup garlic- or Caesar-flavored croutons

¼ cup chopped pitted kalamata olives

2 tablespoons chopped fresh basil

1 clove garlic, minced

2 tablespoons grated Parmesan or Romano cheese

1 tablespoon olive oil

1. Preheat oven to 425°F. Cut tomatoes in half crosswise; discard seeds. Scrape out and reserve pulp. Place tomato shells cut side up in pie plate or baking dish.

2. Chop tomato pulp; place in medium bowl. Add croutons, olives, basil and garlic; mix well. Spoon mixture into tomato shells. Sprinkle with cheese; drizzle with oil.

3. Bake about 10 minutes or until heated through.

SAUTÉED SWISS CHARD

makes 4 servings

1 **large bunch Swiss chard or kale (about 1 pound)**

1 **tablespoon olive oil**

3 **cloves garlic, minced**

¾ **teaspoon salt**

¼ **teaspoon black pepper**

1 **tablespoon balsamic vinegar**

¼ **cup pine nuts, toasted***

*To toast pine nuts, cook in small skillet over medium heat 2 minutes or until lightly browned, stirring frequently.

1. Rinse chard in cold water; shake off excess water but do not dry. Finely chop stems and coarsely chop leaves.

2. Heat oil in large saucepan over medium heat. Add garlic; cook and stir 2 minutes. Add chard, salt and pepper; cover and cook 2 minutes or until chard begins to wilt. Uncover; cook about 5 minutes or until chard is evenly wilted, stirring occasionally.

3. Stir in vinegar. Sprinkle with pine nuts just before serving.

ROASTED PEPPERS AND POTATOES

makes 4 to 6 servings

2 pounds small unpeeled red potatoes, quartered

1 large red bell pepper, cut into 1½-inch pieces

1 large yellow or orange bell pepper, cut into 1½-inch pieces

1 large red onion, cut into 1-inch pieces

¼ cup olive oil

3 cloves garlic, minced

¾ teaspoon salt

¼ teaspoon black pepper

¼ teaspoon dried basil

¼ teaspoon dried oregano

1. Preheat oven to 375°F.

2. Combine potatoes, bell peppers and onion in large resealable food storage bag. Whisk oil, garlic, salt, black pepper, basil and oregano in small bowl; pour over vegetables in bag. Seal bag; shake until vegetables are evenly coated. Spread in single layer on baking sheet.

3. Roast 50 minutes or until potatoes are tender and beginning to brown, stirring every 15 minutes.

FENNEL BRAISED WITH TOMATO

makes 6 servings

2 bulbs fennel

1 tablespoon olive oil

1 small onion, sliced

1 clove garlic, sliced

4 medium tomatoes, chopped

⅔ cup reduced-sodium vegetable broth or water

3 tablespoons dry white wine or vegetable broth

1 tablespoon chopped fresh marjoram *or* 1 teaspoon dried marjoram

¼ teaspoon salt

¼ teaspoon black pepper

1. Trim stems and bottoms from fennel bulbs, reserving green leafy tops (fronds) for garnish. Cut each bulb lengthwise into four wedges.

2. Heat oil in large skillet over medium heat. Add fennel, onion and garlic; cook about 5 minutes or until onion is soft and translucent, stirring occasionally.

3. Stir in tomatoes, broth, wine, marjoram, salt and pepper; cover and cook about 20 minutes or until fennel is tender. Garnish with reserved fennel fronds.

PARMESAN POLENTA

makes 6 servings

4 cups vegetable or chicken broth

1 small onion, minced

4 cloves garlic, minced

1 tablespoon minced fresh rosemary
   or 1 teaspoon dried rosemary

½ teaspoon salt

1¼ cups yellow cornmeal

6 tablespoons grated Parmesan
   cheese

1 tablespoon olive oil, divided

1. Spray 11×7-inch baking pan with nonstick cooking spray. Spray one side of 7-inch-long sheet of waxed paper with cooking spray.

2. Combine broth, onion, garlic, rosemary and salt in medium saucepan; bring to a boil over high heat. Gradually add cornmeal, stirring constantly. Reduce heat to medium; cook 30 minutes or until mixture has consistency of thick mashed potatoes, stirring frequently. Remove from heat; stir in cheese.

3. Spread polenta evenly in prepared pan. Place waxed paper on polenta, sprayed side down, and smooth surface. (If surface is bumpy, it is more likely to stick to the grill.) Cool on wire rack 15 minutes or until firm. Remove waxed paper; cut into six squares.

4. Prepare grill for direct cooking. Spray grid with cooking spray. Brush tops of polenta squares with half of oil. Grill polenta, oil side down, covered, over medium-low heat 6 to 8 minutes or until golden brown. Brush with remaining oil; turn and grill 6 to 8 minutes or until golden brown Serve warm.

ASPARAGUS RISOTTO

makes 6 to 8 servings

5½ cups vegetable broth

⅛ teaspoon salt

4 tablespoons (½ stick) butter, divided

⅓ cup finely chopped onion

2 cups uncooked arborio rice

⅔ cup dry white wine

2½ cups fresh asparagus pieces (about 1 inch)

⅔ cup frozen peas

1 cup grated Parmesan cheese

Shaved Parmesan cheese (optional)

1. Heat broth and salt to a boil in medium saucepan over medium-high heat. Keep warm over low heat.

2. Meanwhile, melt 3 tablespoons butter in large saucepan over medium heat. Add onion; cook and stir 3 minutes or until tender. Add rice; cook 2 minutes or until rice is translucent and coated with butter, stirring frequently. Add wine; cook until most of wine is absorbed, stirring occasionally.

3. Add 1½ cups hot broth; cook and stir 6 to 7 minutes or until most of liquid is absorbed. (Mixture should simmer but not boil.) Add 2 cups broth and asparagus; cook and stir 6 to 7 minutes or until most of liquid is absorbed. Add remaining 2 cups broth and peas; cook and stir 5 to 6 minutes or until most of liquid is absorbed and rice mixture is creamy.

4. Remove from heat; stir in remaining 1 tablespoon butter and 1 cup grated Parmesan. Garnish with shaved Parmesan.

ASPARAGUS–SPINACH RISOTTO: Substitute 1 cup baby spinach or chopped fresh spinach for the peas. Proceed as directed.

ASPARAGUS–CHICKEN RISOTTO: Add 2 cups chopped or shredded cooked chicken to the risotto with the peas in step 3. Proceed as directed.

STUFFED PORTOBELLOS

makes 4 servings

1 tablespoon olive oil

½ cup diced red bell pepper

½ cup diced onion

¼ teaspoon salt

¼ teaspoon dried thyme

⅛ teaspoon black pepper

⅔ cup panko bread crumbs

⅔ cup diced fresh tomatoes or drained canned diced tomatoes

¼ cup grated Parmesan cheese

¼ cup chopped fresh parsley

4 portobello mushroom caps

1. Preheat oven to 375°F.

2. Heat oil in medium nonstick skillet over medium-high heat. Add bell pepper and onion; cook and stir 5 minutes or until vegetables are tender and lightly browned. Stir in salt, thyme and black pepper.

3. Combine vegetable mixture, panko, tomatoes, cheese and parsley in medium bowl; mix well. Place mushrooms, cap sides down, in shallow baking dish. Mound vegetable mixture on mushrooms.

4. Bake 15 minutes or until mushrooms are tender and filling is golden brown.

CARAMELIZED ONION FOCACCIA

makes 12 servings

2 tablespoons plus 1 teaspoon olive oil, divided

1 loaf (16 ounces) frozen bread dough, thawed

4 onions, halved and thinly sliced

½ teaspoon salt

2 tablespoons water

1 tablespoon chopped fresh rosemary

¼ teaspoon black pepper

1 cup (4 ounces) shredded fontina cheese

¼ cup grated Parmesan cheese

1. Brush 13×9-inch baking pan with 1 teaspoon oil. Roll out dough into 13×9-inch rectangle on lightly floured surface. Place in prepared pan; cover and let rise in warm place 30 minutes.

2. Heat remaining 2 tablespoons oil in large skillet over medium-high heat. Add onions and salt; cook 10 minutes or until onions begin to brown, stirring occasionally. Stir in water. Reduce heat to medium; partially cover and cook 20 minutes or until onions are deep golden brown, stirring occasionally. Remove from heat; stir in rosemary and pepper. Let cool slightly.

3. Preheat oven to 375°F. Prick dough all over (about 12 times) with fork. Sprinkle fontina over dough; top with caramelized onions. Sprinkle with Parmesan.

4. Bake 18 to 20 minutes or until golden brown. Remove from pan to wire rack. Cut into pieces; serve warm.

WINTER SQUASH RISOTTO

makes 4 to 6 servings

2 tablespoons olive oil

1 small butternut squash, peeled and cut into 1-inch pieces (about 2 cups)

1 large shallot or small onion, finely chopped

½ teaspoon paprika

¼ teaspoon dried thyme

¼ teaspoon salt

¼ teaspoon black pepper

1 cup uncooked arborio rice

¼ cup dry white wine (optional)

4 to 5 cups hot vegetable broth

½ cup grated Parmesan or Romano cheese

1. Heat oil in large nonstick skillet over medium heat. Add squash; cook and stir 3 minutes. Add shallot; cook and stir 3 to 4 minutes or until squash is almost tender. Stir in paprika, thyme, salt and pepper. Add rice; stir to coat.

2. Add wine, if desired; cook and stir until wine is absorbed. Add broth, ½ cup at a time, stirring frequently until broth is absorbed before adding next ½ cup. Continue adding broth and stirring until rice is tender and mixture is creamy (20 to 25 minutes).

3. Sprinkle with cheese just before serving.

ROASTED BALSAMIC ASPARAGUS >

makes 6 servings

1 pound fresh asparagus

1 tablespoon olive oil

½ teaspoon salt

¼ teaspoon black pepper

1 tablespoon balsamic glaze*

¼ cup shredded or grated Parmesan cheese

Grated lemon peel (optional)

*Balsamic glaze can be found in the condiment section of the supermarket or can be prepared by simmering 2 tablespoons balsamic vinegar until reduced by about half.

1. Preheat oven to 375°F.

2. Arrange asparagus in single layer in shallow 11×7-inch baking dish or on baking sheet. Drizzle with oil; roll gently to coat. Sprinkle with salt and pepper.

3. Roast 14 to 16 minutes or until asparagus is crisp-tender. Drizzle with balsamic glaze; roll again with tongs to coat. Top with cheese; garnish with lemon peel.

QUICK GREEN BEANS WITH ALMONDS

makes 4 servings

1 pound fresh green beans, trimmed

2 tablespoons olive oil

2 teaspoons balsamic vinegar

½ teaspoon salt

¼ teaspoon black pepper

2 tablespoons sliced almonds, toasted*

*To toast almonds, cook in small skillet over medium heat 3 to 5 minutes or until fragrant, stirring frequently.

1. Place beans in medium saucepan; cover with water. Bring to a simmer over high heat. Reduce heat to low; cook 4 to 8 minutes or until beans are crisp-tender. Drain well; return to saucepan.

2. Add oil, vinegar, salt and pepper; toss to coat. Sprinkle with almonds.

DESSERTS

TIRAMISU

makes 9 servings

¾ **cup sugar**

4 **egg yolks**

1 **cup plus 2 tablespoons whipping cream, divided**

16 **ounces mascarpone cheese**

½ **teaspoon vanilla**

¾ **cup cold strong brewed coffee**

¼ **cup coffee-flavored liqueur**

24 **to 28 ladyfingers**

2 **teaspoons unsweetened cocoa powder**

1. Fill medium saucepan half full with water; bring to a boil over high heat. Reduce heat to low to maintain a simmer. Whisk sugar, egg yolks and 2 tablespoons cream in medium metal bowl until well blended. Place bowl over simmering water; cook 6 to 8 minutes or until thickened, whisking constantly. Remove from heat; cool slightly. Whisk in mascarpone and vanilla until smooth and well blended.

2. Pour remaining 1 cup cream into large bowl of electric stand mixer; beat at high speed until stiff peaks form. Gently fold whipped cream into mascarpone mixture until no streaks of white remain.

3. Combine coffee and liqueur in shallow bowl; mix well. Working with one at a time, dip ladyfingers briefly in coffee mixture; arrange in single layer in 9-inch square baking pan, trimming cookies to fit as necessary. Spread thin layer of custard over ladyfingers, covering completely. Dip remaining ladyfingers in remaining coffee mixture; arrange in single layer over custard. Spread remaining custard over cookies. Place cocoa in fine-mesh strainer; sprinkle over custard. Refrigerate 2 hours or overnight.

OAT, CHOCOLATE AND HAZELNUT BISCOTTI

makes about 48 biscotti

1½ **cups whole wheat flour**

1 **cup all-purpose flour**

1 **cup old-fashioned oats**

2 **teaspoons baking powder**

½ **teaspoon salt**

½ **teaspoon ground cinnamon**

1½ **cups sugar**

½ **cup (1 stick) butter, softened**

3 **eggs**

1 **teaspoon vanilla**

2 **cups toasted hazelnuts (see Tip)**

¾ **cup semisweet chocolate chunks**

1. Preheat oven to 325°F. Line cookie sheet with parchment paper. Combine whole wheat flour, all-purpose flour, oats, baking powder, salt and cinnamon in large bowl; mix well.

2. Beat sugar and butter in large bowl with electric mixer at high speed until light and fluffy. Beat in eggs and vanilla until well blended. Gradually beat in flour mixture at low speed just until blended. Stir in hazelnuts and chocolate chunks.

3. Divide dough in half. Shape each half into 10- to 12-inch log; flatten slightly to 3-inch width. Place on prepared cookie sheet.

4. Bake 30 minutes. Cool completely on cookie sheet. *Reduce oven temperature to 300°F.* Transfer logs to cutting board; cut diagonally into ½-inch slices with serrated knife. Arrange slices, cut sides up, on cookie sheet. Bake 10 to 15 minutes or until golden brown. Turn slices; bake 5 to 10 minutes or until golden brown. Remove to wire racks to cool completely.

TIP: To toast hazelnuts, spread on a baking sheet; bake 325°F 5 to 7 minutes. Place nuts in a clean kitchen towel; rub to remove skins.

POLENTA APRICOT PUDDING CAKE

makes 8 servings

¼	cup chopped dried apricots	⅔	cup cornmeal
1½	cups orange juice	½	cup all-purpose flour
1	cup ricotta cheese	½	teaspoon salt
3	tablespoons honey	¼	teaspoon ground nutmeg
¾	cup sugar	½	cup slivered almonds

1. Preheat oven to 325°F. Spray 9-inch nonstick springform pan with nonstick cooking spray.

2. Soak apricots in warm water in small bowl 15 minutes to soften. Drain and pat dry.

3. Beat orange juice, ricotta and honey in large bowl with electric mixer at medium speed 5 minutes or until smooth. Combine sugar, cornmeal, flour, salt and nutmeg in medium bowl; mix well. Add to orange juice mixture; stir until blended. Stir in apricots. Pour into prepared pan; sprinkle with almonds.

4. Bake 40 to 50 minutes or until center is almost set and cake is golden brown. Serve warm.

WARM APPLE CROSTATA

makes 4 tarts (4 to 8 servings)

1¾ cups all-purpose flour

⅓ cup granulated sugar

½ teaspoon plus ⅛ teaspoon salt, divided

¾ cup (1½ sticks) cold butter, cut into small pieces

3 tablespoons ice water

2 teaspoons vanilla

8 Pink Lady or Honeycrisp apples (about 1½ pounds), peeled and cut into ¼-inch slices

¼ cup packed brown sugar

1 tablespoon lemon juice

1 teaspoon ground cinnamon

⅛ teaspoon ground nutmeg

4 teaspoons butter, cut into small pieces

1 egg, beaten

1 to 2 teaspoons coarse sugar

Vanilla ice cream

Caramel ice cream topping

1. Combine flour, granulated sugar and ½ teaspoon salt in food processor; process 5 seconds. Add ¾ cup cold butter; process about 10 seconds or until mixture resembles coarse crumbs.

2. Combine ice water and vanilla in small bowl. With motor running, pour mixture through feed tube; process 12 seconds or until dough begins to come together. Shape dough into a disc; wrap in plastic wrap and refrigerate 30 minutes.

3. Meanwhile, combine apples, brown sugar, lemon juice, cinnamon, nutmeg and remaining ⅛ teaspoon salt in large bowl; toss to coat. Preheat oven to 400°F.

4. Line two baking sheets with parchment paper. Cut dough into four pieces; roll out each piece into 7-inch circle on floured surface. Place on prepared baking sheets; mound apples in center of dough circles (about 1 cup apples for each crostata). Fold or roll up edges of dough towards center to create rim of crostata. Dot apples with 4 teaspoons butter. Brush dough with egg; sprinkle dough and apples with coarse sugar.

5. Bake about 20 minutes or until apples are tender and crust is golden brown. Serve warm topped with ice cream and caramel topping.

ITALIAN CHOCOLATE PIE ALLA LUCIA

makes 8 servings

¼ cup pine nuts

3 tablespoons packed brown sugar

1 tablespoon grated orange peel

1 unbaked 9-inch pie crust

4 ounces bittersweet chocolate, coarsely chopped

3 tablespoons butter

1 can (5 ounces) evaporated milk

3 eggs

3 tablespoons hazelnut liqueur

1 teaspoon vanilla

Whipped cream (optional)

Chocolate curls (optional)

1. Toast pine nuts in dry nonstick skillet over medium heat until golden brown and aromatic, stirring constantly. Finely chop pine nuts; cool to room temperature. Combine pine nuts, brown sugar and orange peel in small bowl; mix well. Sprinkle onto bottom of pie crust; press gently into crust.

2. Preheat oven to 325°F. Melt chocolate and butter in small saucepan over low heat; stir until blended and smooth. Cool to room temperature.

3. Beat chocolate mixture and evaporated milk in medium bowl with electric mixer at medium speed until blended. Add eggs, one at a time, beating well after each addition. Stir in hazelnut liqueur and vanilla. Pour into crust.

4. Bake on center rack of oven 30 to 40 minutes or until set. Cool completely on wire rack. Refrigerate until ready to serve. Top with whipped cream and chocolate curls, if desired.

TIP: To make chocolate curls, melt ½ cup semisweet chocolate chips and 1 teaspoon vegetable oil in a medium microwavable bowl on MEDIUM (50%) 1 minute. Stir until smooth. Spread the chocolate mixture in 2-inch-wide ribbons on a piece of parchment paper. Let stand 1 minute, then use the edge of a spatula to lift and scrape chocolate into curls. Place the curls on a parchment paper-lined baking sheet; let stand until set or refrigerate until ready to use.

CITRUS OLIVE OIL CAKE

makes 10 servings

CAKE

1¾ cups all-purpose flour

1½ cups sugar

1 teaspoon salt

½ teaspoon baking powder

½ teaspoon baking soda

1 cup extra virgin olive oil

1 cup buttermilk

3 eggs

Grated peel and juice of 1 orange

Grated peel and juice of 1 lemon

ORANGE SYRUP

¾ cup orange juice

2 tablespoons sugar

Orange peel strips (optional)

1. Preheat oven to 350°F. Line bottom of 9-inch round baking pan with parchment paper. Spray side of pan and parchment with nonstick cooking spray.

2. For cake, combine flour, 1½ cups sugar, salt, baking powder and baking soda in large bowl; mix well. Whisk oil, buttermilk, eggs, orange peel and juice and lemon peel and juice in medium bowl until well blended. Add to flour mixture; stir until blended. Pour batter into prepared pan.

3. Bake 40 minutes or until top is firm and golden brown and toothpick inserted into center comes out clean. Cool completely in pan on wire rack. Run thin knife around edge of cake to loosen; invert onto serving plate and peel off parchment.

4. For syrup, combine ¾ cup orange juice and 2 tablespoons sugar in small saucepan; bring to a boil over medium-high heat. Reduce heat to medium; cook 10 to 12 minutes or until mixture thickens and is reduced to about ¼ cup. Cool slightly. Pour syrup over cake; cool completely before serving. Garnish with orange peel strips.

LIMONCELLO STRAWBERRY DESSERT >

makes 4 servings

1 **pound fresh strawberries**

1 **cup limoncello (Italian lemon liqueur), divided**

1 **pound cake (10 ounces), cut into 8 slices**

Whipped cream

Shaved chocolate (optional)

Fresh mint leaves (optional)

1. Stem and slice strawberries. Set aside 2 cups sliced strawberries. Coarsely chop remaining strawberries; transfer to medium bowl. Stir in 2 tablespoons limoncello; let stand about 10 minutes.

2. Place two slices cake on each of four dessert plates. Drizzle 1 tablespoon limoncello over each slice.

3. Add sliced strawberries to marinated strawberries; mix gently. Top cake slices with strawberry mixture and whipped cream. Sprinkle with chocolate, if desired; garnish with mint. Serve with remaining limoncello.

COFFEE GRANITA

makes 4 servings

2 **cups strong brewed hot coffee***

½ **cup sugar**

½ **teaspoon vanilla**

*Or use 1½ tablespoons instant coffee stirred into 2 cups boiling water until dissolved.

1. Combine hot coffee, sugar and vanilla in medium bowl or measuring cup; stir until sugar is dissolved.

2. Pour into 8-inch square metal baking pan; cover with foil. Freeze 2 hours or until slushy.

3. Remove from freezer; stir to break up mixture into small chunks. Cover and freeze 2 hours, then stir to break up granita up again. Cover and freeze at least 4 hours or overnight.

4. To serve, scrape surface of granita with large metal spoon to shave off thin pieces. Spoon into individual bowls.

CHOCOLATE HAZELNUT BISCOTTINI

makes 52 biscottini

2½ cups all-purpose flour

1 teaspoon baking powder

½ teaspoon salt

½ teaspoon ground cinnamon

¾ cup (1½ sticks) butter, softened

⅓ cup chocolate-hazelnut spread

¾ cup sugar

2 eggs

1 cup coarsely chopped toasted hazelnuts*

1 cup milk chocolate chips

To toast hazelnuts, cook in small skillet over medium heat 2 minutes or until skins begin to peel and nuts are lightly browned, stirring frequently. Transfer to clean dish towel; rub hazelnuts to remove skins. Cool before using.

1. Line baking sheet with parchment paper. Combine flour, baking powder, salt and cinnamon in medium bowl; mix well.

2. Beat butter and chocolate-hazelnut spread in large bowl with electric mixer at medium speed until light and fluffy. Add sugar; beat until fluffy. Add eggs, one at a time, beating until blended after each addition. Gradually add flour mixture, beating until blended. Add hazelnuts and chocolate chips; beat just until blended.

3. Shape dough into two 13×2-inch strips; gently pat to smooth tops. Refrigerate 3 to 4 hours. Preheat oven to 350°F. Line cookie sheet with parchment paper. Place dough strips on cookie sheet.

4. Bake 25 to 30 minutes or until golden brown and firm. *Reduce oven temperature to 325°F.* Remove cookie strips to cutting board; cool 10 minutes. Cut each strip crosswise into 1-inch slices with serrated knife; cut each slice in half. Arrange pieces on baking sheet, cut sides up. Bake 15 minutes; turn and bake 15 minutes. Cool completely.

METRIC CONVERSION CHART

VOLUME MEASUREMENTS (dry)

1/8 teaspoon = 0.5 mL
1/4 teaspoon = 1 mL
1/2 teaspoon = 2 mL
3/4 teaspoon = 4 mL
1 teaspoon = 5 mL
1 tablespoon = 15 mL
2 tablespoons = 30 mL
1/4 cup = 60 mL
1/3 cup = 75 mL
1/2 cup = 125 mL
2/3 cup = 150 mL
3/4 cup = 175 mL
1 cup = 250 mL
2 cups = 1 pint = 500 mL
3 cups = 750 mL
4 cups = 1 quart = 1 L

VOLUME MEASUREMENTS (fluid)

1 fluid ounce (2 tablespoons) = 30 mL
4 fluid ounces (1/2 cup) = 125 mL
8 fluid ounces (1 cup) = 250 mL
12 fluid ounces (1 1/2 cups) = 375 mL
16 fluid ounces (2 cups) = 500 mL

WEIGHTS (mass)

1/2 ounce = 15 g
1 ounce = 30 g
3 ounces = 90 g
4 ounces = 120 g
8 ounces = 225 g
10 ounces = 285 g
12 ounces = 360 g
16 ounces = 1 pound = 450 g

DIMENSIONS

1/16 inch = 2 mm
1/8 inch = 3 mm
1/4 inch = 6 mm
1/2 inch = 1.5 cm
3/4 inch = 2 cm
1 inch = 2.5 cm

OVEN TEMPERATURES

250°F = 120°C
275°F = 140°C
300°F = 150°C
325°F = 160°C
350°F = 180°C
375°F = 190°C
400°F = 200°C
425°F = 220°C
450°F = 230°C

BAKING PAN SIZES

Utensil	Size in Inches/Quarts	Metric Volume	Size in Centimeters
Baking or Cake Pan (square or rectangular)	8×8×2	2 L	20×20×5
	9×9×2	2.5 L	23×23×5
	12×8×2	3 L	30×20×5
	13×9×2	3.5 L	33×23×5
Loaf Pan	8×4×3	1.5 L	20×10×7
	9×5×3	2 L	23×13×7
Round Layer Cake Pan	8×1½	1.2 L	20×4
	9×1½	1.5 L	23×4
Pie Plate	8×1¼	750 mL	20×3
	9×1¼	1 L	23×3
Baking Dish or Casserole	1 quart	1 L	—
	1½ quart	1.5 L	—
	2 quart	2 L	—